# THE IMPOSSIBLE MENTOR
## FINDING COURAGE TO FOLLOW JESUS

RAY HOLLENBACH

ISBN: 0-9882787-0-7
ISBN-13: 978-0-9882787-0-7

TO KIMBERLI:

my lifetime companion, my one true love, and most trusted
counselor.

# CONTENTS

# ACKNOWLEDGMENTS

The most reliable laboratory for ideas, especially spiritual ideas, is the home. Our children, Joe (and his wife, Laura), Evangeline, and Kate-Lin are examples of patience and long-suffering under their father's instruction. When I had no other audience, they listened--and because I'm never at a loss for words, they listened a lot. May the true Father add jewels to their crown for this kindness alone.

The People of Vineyard Christian Fellowship, Campbellsville, Kentucky, who have lived into these ideas over the past 15 years, and patiently accepted me even when my actions could not attain to my rhetoric. Also the Vineyard Writer's group, who for the last three years have read, parsed, critiqued, and encouraged many of the sections of this work, especially Amy Durham, who proved to be a valuable help in the publishing process.

The Convent (David and Jody Nixon of sustainablefaith.org) deserves special recognition, because the earliest chapters were written there. The Nixons have created a place of centered, peaceful hospitality that helps birth dreams.

Lifelong friends Steve Peifer and Rex Miller, who provided equal measures of encouragement and reality checks. Both are already authors in their own right and deserve a wider audience for their fine works.

The students at Campbellsville University, an earnest liberal arts school in my hometown, have born the unreasonable burden of learning these concepts under the twin threats of testing and grading. Most of them bore their burden well, a few did not. The Dean of Cambellsville's School of Theology, Dr. John Hurtgen, has been a constant encourager, and has taken the heat when his over-zealous adjunct instructor crossed lines of academic propriety (more than once!).

Finally, after citing the wealth of riches above, I have been given the additional treasure of three creative and ministry friends, Adam Russell, Eric Hurtgen, and John Mark McMillan, each have steadfastly urged me forward, and pointed beyond conventional means of communication. Everyone should have friends from another generation, if only for the sheer joy of annoying them.

# PART ONE:
# FOUR PROBLEMS

# CHAPTER ONE
## "I'M NOT JESUS!"

I knew it was a mistake as soon as the words left my mouth. Seated in my office was a young man who had been cheated out of $200 by someone else in our church. Both men attended our church, and one guy really did owe the other $200. But the guilty party wasn't in the office, the victim was--and he was full of anger and frustration because of his loss. He was a Christian who cared enough about his faith to try to settle his grievance within the church. Hired by a contractor in the church, he had worked on a construction site for three days but was never paid. The brother-contractor had run out of money. The longer we talked about possible solutions, the more frustrated he became—after all, he had earned the money.

We talked for a half-hour. I watched his anger grow, and his anger was more damaging than the $200. Finally, I made a suggestion, "You could forgive him his debt," I said. "Jesus told us to do just that."

Big mistake.

"Well, I'm not Jesus!" he shot back. End of discussion, end of ministry time, end of opportunity to take the yoke Jesus offers. It was my mistake. Not for suggesting a perfectly Biblical remedy to his anger, but for expressing the solution in such a way this young believer considered impossible.

**Pursuing the Impossible**

It's impossible to be like Jesus, isn't it? Jesus was perfect. He led a sinless life. He was God-come-to-earth and his life sets the bar impossibly high for any of us. Worship Jesus? Sure. Our modern notions of worship encourage us to pour out our hearts in admiration and affection. Bible studies about Jesus? Definitely. Our Enlightenment mindset reinforces the notion that learning is the highest good. Evangelize for Jesus? Certainly. It's the Great Commission! Even casual observation reveals the need for a savior in every society. But actually become like Jesus? It can't be done.

The reaction of the young man in my office points to a challenge facing Christians today: we are prepared to worship, to study, and to work for Jesus but we lack the conviction that it is possible to become like him. We are human, he is divine. We are flawed, he is perfect.

We are his followers, but who can truly follow him? Even though the Western church has rediscovered discipleship and celebrated spiritual disciplines, there remains in the hearts of believers ambivalence toward promise of becoming like Jesus. Despite the church's social and political engagement with the culture; despite waves of revival and revivalism washing over the land in the last century; and despite the explosion of Christian publishing as a resource for the church worldwide, there is an entrenched conviction that because we are "sinners saved by grace" we can never effectively respond to Jesus's command to "Be perfect, therefore, as your heavenly Father is perfect." (Matthew 5:48) The irony is that while we willingly respond to his call to come and follow we simultaneously prepare our hearts for failure in the task.

Some passages in the Scripture fill us with comfort. Some light the fires of hope in our hearts. Other passages seem too idealistic, too fantastic to find their way into our daily lives or even into our dreams. Those passages that speak of our truly becoming like Jesus are in the second category: "For those God foreknew he also predestined to be conformed to the likeness of his Son, that he might be the firstborn among many brothers." (Romans 8:29) Is this possible? Does God really look at each one of us and see a destiny in which we look like Jesus? In the gospels, Jesus made astounding claims about himself--and his followers. "While I am in the world, I am the light of the world," he said of himself (John 9:5) yet he also taught his disciples, "*You* are the light of the world." (Matthew 5:14, emphasis added) The same Jesus who fed thousands of people from meager resources also told his disciples, "*You* give them something to eat." (John 6:37 emphasis added) The same Jesus who healed the sick and raised the dead sent out his disciples with the very same instructions. (Matthew, chapter 10; Luke, chapters 9 & 10)

When the Apostle Paul wrote to the Galatians he described the anguish he felt over their spiritual formation. "I am again in the pains of childbirth until Christ is formed in you." (4:29) Paul apparently labored under the expectation that those who came to Christ would find themselves changed into the likeness of Christ. As he wrote to the churches he planted, Paul emphasized not only the sacrificial death of Jesus--he also pointed to the example Jesus provided for every follower: "Your attitude should be the same as that of Christ Jesus" (Philippians 2: 5); "We proclaim him, admonishing and teaching everyone with all wisdom, so that we may present everyone perfect in Christ." (Colossians 1: 28); "you have been given fullness in Christ," (Colossians 2:10). Paul made it clear that these Biblical affirmations were not only for individuals, but also for the corporate body that is the church: "until we all reach unity in the faith and in the knowledge of the Son of God and become mature, attaining to the whole measure of the fullness of Christ." (Ephesians 4:13); "that you may know how to behave in the house of God, which is the assembly of the living God, the pillar and foundation of the truth." (I Timothy 3:15)

Whatever our theological foundations regarding these passages, we should recognize that they are about God's intention for each of one us to become "conformed to the likeness of his Son." Simply put, God desires to have more children like Jesus. Jesus is God's only begotten Son, but we become his sons and daughters by adoption. The destiny of those adopted into the family of God is that we, too, should bear the family likeness. That is, we will look like Jesus.

The central problem in nurturing followers of Jesus is our unspoken view of Jesus as the Impossible Mentor. It's a paradox: nearly everyone is willing to acknowledge Jesus is a worthy role model, but almost no one seriously believes it is possible to live up to his example. Our esteem for Jesus does battle with the deep-seated notion that it is impossible to be like him. Why choose a mentor who is impossible to imitate?

## The Great Divide

What are we to do? The revelation of scripture presents the possibility of becoming like Jesus while our everyday experience leads us to believe otherwise. Two responses are commonplace in the church today. One response is to place the fulfillment of our destiny in Christ into the "age to come." It will be his doing upon his return. Second, we affirm the scriptural witness as theologically true while separating it from practice: "this may be the way God sees us," we think, "but it isn't the way we really are." Our interpretive approach emphasizes our "legal standing" before God without addressing our daily choices. The gap between God's heart for us and our shortcomings is bridged by justification ("just-as-if-I'd never sinned"). Everyday life has been separated from the Biblical witness. Everyday life doesn't include Christlikeness. "After all," we reason, "I'm only human."

The average Christian attempts spiritual formation programs with the same confidence as Americans who try the next diet fad—with largely the same results. We affirm that after we have come to him for atonement, he will work within us to change our very nature, but the change is not really effective until we will see him face to face. The arena of change is in heaven.

Over the years I have taught several introductory-level classes in New Testament at a nearby university. When we finish reading the gospels I always ask my students if they think Jesus is a worthy role model. In each class nearly every hand goes up in the affirmative. (Students are smart--they know how to give the instructor the answer he's looking for!) Then I ask my follow-up question: "How many of you think it's possible to live up to his example?" Not a single hand goes up. No one moves. Who in their right mind would claim they could measure up to Jesus? It is one thing to esteem Jesus or even recognize his claim to be God come-to-earth, but who would take on the responsibility to be like him? We affirm him as a role model and simultaneously deny any real possibility of becoming like him. In a conversation with a dozen young Christians recently, I asked them if they felt it was possible to live a life without sin for even one day. No takers. I rephrased the question and asked if it is possible to go an hour without sinning. Only one of them thought it was possible to stay within the will of God for a single hour.

These questions are not academic. They go to the heart of our life "in Christ." If our intuition tells us following His example is impossible, for a day or even one hour, how can we have the confidence to pursue his vision for us? Some go through the motions of discipleship without any hope of effective change; others are intuitively suspicious of spiritual formation as somehow a negation of God's grace. It is all too common for believers to attend meetings, pray, and read their Bibles as a matter of Christian duty without any expectation that their lives could become like Jesus. After all, they were told at conversion that their own efforts could not save them, so why should their efforts after conversion impact their day-to-day lives?

There are other, darker, aspects to our ambivalence about following Jesus. What kind of Master would invite me to be his apprentice if he thought I had no possibility to follow in his footsteps? What kind of God would send his son to Earth, hold him up as the perfect role model, issue a call for his people to follow the son's example--all the while knowing they could never live up to the command to be like Jesus? We are grateful for the gift of eternal life but wary about what God might expect in return--and our inability to fulfill his expectations. Isn't heaven a gift? Isn't this what grace is all about? Jesus is the one who saves; he wouldn't demand anything beyond faith for salvation, would he? Isn't the call to discipleship a "bait and switch" tactic after the promise of eternal life? If Jesus is perfect, and I am called to be like him, doesn't that set me up for failure? If I decide to give discipleship a try, what kind of guilt awaits me when I fail? True, I can be forgiven, but I'll still be a failure.

If we consider him worthy of imitation but secretly hold the conviction that imitation is impossible we have set ourselves up for some serious disharmony. We are encouraged in our Christian walk to look to Jesus as the example, but we are also taught that he is the unique Son of God. We are of two minds, and we would do well to recall the Biblical witness about double-mindedness. James tells us that the double-minded man is "unstable in all his ways." (James 1:8)

Perhaps our double-mindedness expresses itself in the cycle of attempting discipleship, spiritual disciplines, and holiness on the one hand, and failure (with the attendant guilt) on the other. Instability is the mark of Christians who admire Jesus but cannot bring themselves to put his words into practice. In this first chapter of his letter, James continues this line of thought to an often-overlooked conclusion: "He chose to give us birth through the word of truth, that we might be a kind of firstfruits of all he created."

(James 1:18) The idea is that followers of Jesus should be the example of what a new creation looks like. James wrote to those who were already believers, not to the "lost." He encouraged followers of Jesus to live in a tangibly different manner from the rest of the world, the "old creation." The issues he raised in his letter concerned the need for wisdom and the application of faith in a manner that brought visible results, the kind of results that would give hope to a watching world.

### Someone Else, Maybe?

If we are overwhelmed by the call to imitate the Lord Himself, then perhaps we could find a more accessible role model? We might be tempted to choose another mentor, a pastor, a friend, a celebrity, or an "older brother." For those tempted in this direction James had a remarkable suggestion: consider Elijah. "The prayer of a righteous man is powerful and effective. Elijah was a man just like us. He prayed earnestly that it would not rain, and it did not rain on the land for three and a half years. Again he prayed, and the heavens gave rain, and the earth produced its crops." (James 5: 16b – 18) James, the brother of the Lord Jesus, surely must have struggled with the disparity between his actions and those of Jesus, yet he closes his letter with a suggestion that would seem unattainable by most believers today. Who is greater, Jesus, or Elijah? Of course, we know the answer. Shouldn't Elijah's life of faith and practice be more attainable than that of Jesus?

"Elijah was a man just like us." How many of us believe that? Elijah's life story involves a supernatural prayer life capable of changing weather patterns. Elijah was a man like us? He was subject to uncertainty, perhaps even bouts with depression. These similarities resonate with us, but he also miraculously multiplied food, called down fire from heaven, and raised the dead. If James seriously attempted to lower the bar by suggesting a mere human as a mentor, in our day we are still left standing and staring at the height of the bar. Elijah's life certainly has the authority of scripture, but how are we to understand, interpret or adapt his life to our experience? What would be the response of family and friends if we maintained that we were just like Elijah? Yet we know we are called to follow Jesus, not Elijah. As we read James' instructions to the early church, what level of expectation should we have?

God has a greater vision for what is possible in our lives than we do. Perhaps the reason the Apostle Paul instructs us in Romans to "be transformed by the renewing of your minds" (Romans 12:2) is so we can see the possibilities of a life lived in harmony with Jesus. There is a practical, day-to-day, moment-by-moment harmony capable of generating the rest and peace he promises. "Come to me, all you who are weary and burdened, and I will give you rest. Take my yoke upon you and learn from me, for I am gentle and humble in heart, and you will find rest for your souls. For my yoke is easy and my burden is light." (Matthew 11:28–30) Beyond rest and peace are the staggering possibilities of living a life imitating Jesus in word, thought, attitude and deed. Jesus invites us to learn from him because he intends to reproduce himself in us. He does not invite us to learn *about* him; he presents to each of the incredible offer to become *conformed* to his image.

Like the young man from the beginning of the chapter who was cheated out of his paycheck, we have the opportunity to take the yoke Jesus offers. This young man was a construction worker, an occupation not so different from Jesus's years as a carpenter. Did my young friend ever meditate on the years Jesus spent as a "working man?" Even a modest imagination could conceive of a situation where Jesus may have been denied a wage he had earned. The difficulty in asking the question, "what would Jesus do" comes not in imagining a possible answer, but in seeing ourselves as capable of imitating his actions. (By the way, after our meeting I telephoned the contractor who owed the money, who was also a member of our church. He was surprised to hear from his pastor about the impasse! He told me it would be a few months before his company would be profitable again, and assured me he would pay the wages he owed. When I suggested that he consider selling his expensive pick-up truck, buying an older, used model and using the difference to pay the wages, he decided to go to another church.) We must choose whether becoming like Jesus is possible in this life, or even desirable. If we decide that becoming like Jesus is not possible, we can avoid facing the more difficult question of whether it is desirable.

In his earthly ministry Jesus used everyday situations to shape his disciples: paying taxes, feeding the hungry, fishing, encountering a fever at home, settling disputes between people filled with pride and competition. Jesus knew that commonplace situations contained eternal possibilities: a drink of water could change a town, coins could become cities, and palm leaves could threaten an empire. Moreover, Jesus expected to leave behind a group of followers who were capable of continuing his work in every respect. His solutions transformed the most unlikely cast of characters into world-changers who operated with his priorities, lived out his example, and operated with the same authority and power as their Master.

## Getting Started

Where can we begin in the pursuit of an apprenticeship with the Master? Is it possible to follow Jesus? How can we practically take his yoke upon our selves? How does Biblical discipleship differ from academic study or professional internship in the religion industry? Questions like these must be raised before discipleship or spiritual formation can be attempted.

Each of the following points present opportunities for prayer, meditation, and reflection. Most Christians know the correct answer, but the more important consideration is whether we *believe* the correct answer:

Is it possible to learn from him? Some settings promote learning about Jesus, others facilitate learning from him; there is a world of difference between the two. How will I know the difference between them? Is it possible?

If Jesus is my mentor, have I committed myself to failure with no possibility of success? Here we must examine our foundations, not his. In the world of athletics, no coach wants his players to step into the arena convinced of defeat. How do we define success when our calling is to imitate the perfect sinless Son of God? More important, how does *he* define success?

What expectation does Jesus have regarding my relationship with him? In his earthly ministry Jesus modeled a life of obedience to the Father and discipleship of his followers. He mentored twelve diverse men. Does Jesus still disciple his followers twenty centuries later? How does he accomplish his task in our time? What is his role and how can I relate to him?

How will he shape me? What is his vision for my life? What is the role of the Scripture in the master's training program? What is the role of the church? The Holy Spirit? What is my role?

These questions must be faced before we begin. The answers spoken from our intellect will not help us. The answers spoken from our heart will determine whether discipleship is possible.

# CHAPTER TWO
## YOU'RE NOT, EITHER

The class held about thirty students. A class that size guarantees a mix of sleepers, zombies, texters and those rare few who participate in discussion. We had spent the whole hour talking about the words of Jesus, "Be perfect as your Heavenly Father is perfect." Could Jesus possibly be serious about this? One student seemed to pay particular attention but hadn't spoken up once during the period. I decided to draw her into the discussion.

"So we're just about done for today. Tiffanie, you've been listening hard but haven't offered your opinion. Why don't you have the last word?"

She shifted in her seat and said, "I don't know if he was serious, but one thing's for sure: you ain't Jesus."

## Who is Qualified?

Our inability to connect with Jesus as the model for our lives has two immediate consequences. First, all other Christian role models pale in comparison to the perfect Son of God: since no one measures up to the Master, no one is qualified to lead us. Regarding our own behavior we are tempted to say, "I'm not Jesus." When we encounter another believer who could possibly become an example for us the same defense mechanism rises up to say, "You're not, either." Second, because earthly mentors are fallible we have trained ourselves to keep our guard up, to remain at a distance. There are too many examples of fallen Christian leaders. We are determined not to be drawn into a close relationship with those who could nurture us into Christlikeness, because they could also let us down. So we end up with no role models at all.

Beware the pastor who plays on your church-league softball team. Or basketball. Or horseshoes. You will discover that your pastor has character flaws like the Jordan River, deep and wide. If he is athletic he is likely to be considered too competitive, and if he is not athletic he likely doesn't take the game seriously enough. We started a church softball team at our church in order to encourage the value of community--and ended up losing two families by the end of the season!

If we have difficulty embracing the flawless Son of God as our life coach, then an accessible human mentor would seem to be just the ticket. Unfortunately Christian leaders are at a real disadvantage when compared to Jesus. We are left with imperfect leaders whose flaws are available daily for inspection. Most people will pay lip service to the idea that there is "no perfect leader," but when the flaws begin to show through, lip service gives way to disappointment, hurt feelings, and criticism. This is the second challenge to taking the yoke that Jesus offers. The Christian who hears the call to discipleship is faced with two difficult choices in looking for a mentor. First, Jesus is the Impossible Mentor; second, most Christian leaders are Unqualified Mentors. The church is left with no mentors at all.

Even within the church, leaders are unwilling to step forward to disciple others. For example, in my youth I was a diver on my high school swimming team. Like most teenagers I had taught myself how to do a front flip and a back flip, but going beyond the basics required coaching. The next step was to learn how to do one-and-a-half summersaults and land in the water headfirst. My coach was another high schooler, a senior, who was a great diver. I asked him about doing the one-and-a-half. I wanted to understand the concept and to know what to expect. His answer was surprising. "You just throw your head down into the water," he said. "You just have to feel it. Here, I'll show you," and in what seemed like one graceful move he was up in the air, tumbling easily and knifing the water. He didn't know physics or aerodynamics. He didn't know the technical terms of diving. But he could show me how. I learned how to do one-and-a half summersaults as a freshman, and by my senior year I could do two-and-a-half summersaults. In my first year of diving I was a disciple of someone who knew how to dive. He was older, more experienced, and he demonstrated how to dive day by day. In less religious language, he was my coach, my mentor, my example. He taught me how to be a diver and to this day, decades later, I can still do one-and-a-half summersaults.

That same freshman year in high school I became a follower of Jesus. I knew I needed to learn a new way to live because my life was a mess. But unlike my diving career, it took me years to find an example for following Jesus. "Don't look at me," my church youth-leader said. "I'm just a man. Keep your eyes on Jesus." This presented a problem for me because I couldn't see Jesus. I could read about him. I was certain that his sacrifice paid the debt for my sin. I just couldn't see how in the world I would ever be like him. The problem was Jesus was unreachable. To make matters worse, everyone I knew kept pointing only to him. In the earliest days of my Christian walk I heard the same words over and over again, "keep your eyes on Jesus." If the advice for Christian growth ever deviated from "don't follow me, I'm just a man," the only other message I received was, "be sure to read your Bible and pray." I tried to do it, but prayer was boring and lifeless. Bible reading was a little more interesting--and also a lot more confusing.

In my experience as a young Christian, leaders in the church seemed to indicate that we were all in the same boat, leaders and church members alike: sinners who needed a Savior. As a new believer I got the message; but the problem was that I was already in the boat--I was looking for someone to show me how to become a useful part of the crew.

Over the decades I discovered that most youth leaders and pastors were unwilling to step forward and suggest that they can teach people how to become conformed to the image of Christ. In church after church the substance of sermon after sermon was either our need for a savior or our responsibilities to live up to the commandments we find in the Bible. The how-to of Christian living was strangely missing.

## "Imitate Me"

Then, one day, almost by accident, I came across an amazing statement by the Apostle Paul. It startled me because it was so different from what I was used to hearing in church. This man, Paul, said: "Be imitators of me, just as I also am of Christ." (1 Corinthians 11:1) Paul seemed to be confident in his relationship with Jesus. Although he once referred to himself as "the worst of sinners," he claimed to know what was required to follow Jesus and invited people to imitate his actions. Instantly I knew I needed exactly this: someone to imitate. Jesus was still the goal, but Paul was someone who did something more than simply point to the goal. He told the Corinthians, "Here. I'll show you how."

How many Christians (or even leaders in the church) make such statements today? I suspect that many people would consider Paul's words boastful if they heard someone else say them. Yet this is exactly what Jesus instructed his followers in the Great Commission when he charged his disciples with making more disciples, and to "teach them to observe everything I have commanded you." (Matthew 28:20) I believe this is the second challenge for those who want to become followers of Jesus. We have a gospel that promotes forgiveness and exalts Jesus as Savior. We have

Biblical language that exalts Jesus as Lord. We do not, however, have much of an idea about how to make disciples who will actually become like Jesus.

In fact, many leaders consider discipleship to be secondary to preaching the gospel. I have heard this kind of statement more than once from the pulpit: "When you get to heaven God will only have two questions. 'Do you know my Son?' and, 'How many did you bring with you?'" I would like to suggest that this concern for evangelism is sincere but misguided. Even for those whose hearts burn to win the lost, the proper response should be to follow Jesus' instruction to make disciples.

Each of us should ask, "Is my life worthy of imitating?" This question is difficult to ask if we believe that we cannot possibly live up to his example. It is doubly difficult to ask if we believe the idea that no one else is qualified teach us how to live up to his example.

In the gospels Jesus' message was the good news of the Kingdom of God, and his Kingdom method included *making disciples*. Just 15 verses into Mark's gospel Jesus announced, "The time has come. The kingdom of God is near. Repent and believe the good news!" (Mark 1:15) Immediately—in the next four verses--he called four men to come and follow him. The Kingdom proclamation and the command to come and follow cannot be separated. From the very earliest moments of his ministry Jesus called men to follow him. It was the call of the Kingdom and it was his invitation into his school of ministry.

After Jesus finished his mission, the inspired record of the book of Acts shows nearly every believer doing ministry. Even as Acts depicts the rise of leaders within the church, it also reveals everyday believers doing the works of Jesus and proclaiming the Kingdom of God. Acts contains stories of men like Stephen, Philip, and Ananias chapter after chapter (Acts 7, 8, & 9), those who were not Apostles, men who were ordinary believers doing Kingdom works. The growing church needed leaders, to be sure, but it appears that the Scripture does not set apart ministry as an activity reserved only for leaders. When did ministry become a task exclusive to leaders?

**Ministry School:**

In the centuries that followed the book of Acts, the church endeavored to develop various schools of ministry, schools which attempted to qualify who was able to do the work of the ministry. The church has drawn from Greek models of philosophy. Next it used military models and business models. The church looked to educational models and developed universities and seminaries. But something has been lost (or largely lost) in formal methods to equip people for ministry. What's been lost is the Jesus-curriculum for a school of ministry, a school that should be required for all followers of Jesus. Rarely has the church imitated the example of Jesus and simply repeated his call, "Come follow me." (To be fair, there have been communities throughout the centuries who have not lost the Jesus method: for example the Waldensians of the 12th century, the Moravians of the 18th century, or the "Back to Jerusalem" movement of Chinese house churches in our day.)

Most especially in our modern era—an age which values accreditation and authorization—the church looks skeptically on those who would attempt to do ministry apart from specialized training or recognition conferred by others. And not without reason: one doesn't need to look very far to find people who have been harmed ministry done badly. But somewhere along the way we have lost sight of the wise and simple pattern laid down by the Master: come and follow and I will teach you to do the things I do. In turn, you will go out and make more disciples.

Jesus selected tradesmen and villagers to follow him. In the act of following they became fit to do his work and to train others to do his work. They learned his ways not through formal education but by being with him and imitating him. When Mark's gospel presents a list of the disciples it states simply that Jesus chose them "that they might be with him and he might send them out..." (Mark 3: 14). The pre-eminent qualification for ministry was that they were with him. In plain language the scripture reveals a very simple pattern: be with Jesus (discipleship), then go out at his direction (disciple-making). Even those who criticized the earliest disciples observed, "these men had been with Jesus." (Acts 4:13) It's not difficult to imagine. These men traveled with Jesus, camped and ate with Jesus, and shared life with him. If he was invited to a wedding, they went with him. If he taught the masses, they were with him. If he stayed up most of the night healing the sick, they were with him. It was their constant exposure to his presence and activity that became their school of ministry. Jesus did not assign readings or lecture extensively. If they had questions about what he said publicly, they asked him privately. And if Jesus had a concern about their behavior he asked them about it (for example, Mark 8:17).

It is worth noting that with respect to preparation for ministry, neither Jesus nor any of his original twelve disciples would be considered qualified to teach in a university or seminary today! Our educational biases tilt strongly toward knowing *about* Jesus or *about* the scriptures as opposed to *knowing him or being with him.* Objective knowledge is certainly easier to quantify, but Jesus seemed to care far more about imitation and relationship than formal education. Clearly he and his disciples valued the scriptures, and all of them demonstrated knowledge of the scripture, but these abilities were secondary to relationship with Jesus.

**Step One: Come. Step Two, Follow:**

Here is a challenge to our understanding of Jesus and his value system: after sending 70 of his followers out for their first ministry experience, he rejoiced before the Father with these words: "I praise you, Father, Lord of heaven and earth, because you have hidden these things from the wise and learned, and revealed them to little children. Yes, Father, for this was your good pleasure. " (Luke 10:21) What are we to make of this? Jesus rejoiced that the wise and the learned did not have access to knowledge of God's ways!

Jesus summed up the entire curriculum for training his disciples with a simple command, "Come, follow me." For many of us "Come follow me" is too simple. Jesus is no longer here, how can we follow? Jesus lived in another place and time, how does his life serve as an example for ours today? Or perhaps the greatest challenge: Jesus is the sinless Son of God, isn't it impossible to follow him?

Perhaps the very fact that we stumble at the invitation demonstrates why individual Christians (and the church as a whole) have difficulty impacting our society. We are good at study. We are big at planning and organizing. We are very good at structure and control. But we are not very good at following. Those who cannot grasp "Come follow me" as a method of training underscore the problems we face. I suspect that we are limited in our effectiveness because we have placed understanding above obedience. We have prized our intellectual capacities above the kind of love that causes us to become imitators of the Beloved. Little children love their parents and imitate all their actions; it is the time of their greatest development. "I am the way and the truth and the life," Jesus said. "No one comes to the Father except through me." (John 14:6) Jesus did not say, "I know the answer," he said "I am the way." He did not say, "I know the truth," he said "I am the truth." And he did not say "I will teach you about the life," and said, "I am the Life." Jesus did not come to produce *agree-ers*, he came to produce followers.

Some may object that since Jesus is no longer involved in earthly ministry that the model had to change. But he himself said, "I only do the things I see the Father doing." (John 5:19) He demonstrated how to follow an invisible God. He showed us how it is done. His actions present a clear pattern for us to follow. This is our first opportunity to follow him. When Jesus ascended to heaven he left behind an invaluable resource: people who knew how to follow him. These unschooled men became the resource for teaching the church. Their method of instruction was to lead by example. This is our second opportunity to follow him, by imitating the example of godly Christians. When we reject the possibility that flawed men can provide an example worth imitating, we reject the very model Jesus left behind.

The gospels combine these two opportunities into the Biblical model for discipleship. Jesus chose deeply flawed individuals as his followers, and prepared these imperfect men to become disciple-makers in his absence. When we turn the page from the gospels to the book of Acts we encounter the very same men who were so clueless just weeks before. They had been with Jesus, they were empowered by the Holy Spirit on the day of Pentecost, but they still did not have all the answers and they still contained character flaws. The earliest Christian leaders had significant personality issues. Peter demonstrated boldness in front of the religious authorities and yet was timid within the fellowship of the earliest church (compare Acts 3 with Galatians 2). The Apostle Paul clashed with Peter publicly, and also had a major difference of opinion with Barnabas regarding the staff for a missionary trip. The split between Paul and Barnabas is significant with respect to personal weaknesses: Barnabas was a decades-long friend of Paul, his greatest supporter, in fact. The very name Barnabas was an affectionate label that meant "son of encouragement," how could Paul throw this relationship away? Yet these were the very men whom God used to disciple the next generation of believers. The fact that these men were something less than the perfect Son of God did not disqualify them from making disciples. In our frame of reference, when we see personality flaws in others we reject them as worthy mentors. When we acknowledge our own weaknesses we consider ourselves disqualified from making disciples.

### Drop-dead Leadership?

Within the first-century church the Holy Spirit held people to a high standard of integrity, but not sinless perfection. The most serious offense was hypocrisy. Consider the fate of two disciples who tried to appear "better" than they actually were—Ananias and Sapphira (Acts, chapter five). Can you imagine a modern-day equivalent? What would be the modern public reaction to a Christian leader who confronted hypocrisy in the church, only to have the deceivers fall dead at his feet? I'm certainly not suggesting a return to those days, but we should stop long enough to note that this sensational event did not create a leadership crisis in the early church. Quite the contrary: it further established the leadership.

Our reluctance to become a disciple of the Impossible Mentor is the beginning of our problems in spiritual formation. This reluctance has bled over into a reluctance to follow others, precisely because they are not perfect. It is easier, we reason, to retreat into Biblical study and methods of growth that are not built upon relationships. Biblical knowledge is important but impersonal—the exact opposite of the Word made flesh. The scripture is a divinely inspired and sovereignly protected gift from God to the church, but it is easier to relate to a book than a Person. When we distance ourselves from the living Lord and from the presence of the Holy Spirit in others and retreat into study, we do so at our peril.

## CHAPTER THREE
## PARALYZED BY GRACE

A few years ago I had to find another doctor. My previous one couldn't help me. He was able to diagnose the problem, but not suggest a remedy that would fix things once and for all. I kept going back to him week after week. My appointments began to sound like an old vaudeville routine:

*"Your problem is: you're sick."*

*"Of course I'm sick," I replied. "That's why I'm here."*

*"Have you had this before?" he'd ask.*

*"You know I've had this before. I had it the last time I was here."*

*"Well, you've got it again."*

*I tried demonstrating the problem: "It hurts when I do this."*

*"Well, don't do that."*

*"Doctor, is there any hope for me?"*

*"Of course there is. Take two aspirin. You'll feel better when you're dead."*

Of course, I made that up. But many of us have been returning to the same place, year after year, with the same problem. We are offered the same solution and we leave feeling as if there should be a better remedy available, but the professional assures us that we are on the right track. If you haven't guessed already, the professional is not a doctor but a pastor, and the doctor's office is our regular gathering for church. We go to church only to experience what Yogi Berra called "Déjà vu all over again." We are reminded of our sin and God's grace toward that sin.

And this is correct: we *are* sinful. Jesus' sacrifice on the cross paid the price for our redemption. And of course the grace of God should be celebrated and declared by the church. But grace—understood as the one-time event of redemption—is not the sole message of the church nor the full content of the gospel of the Kingdom of God. Church-goers commonly experience the drama of forgiveness each week, or hear the gospel presented again and again as the call of God to wayward sinners to make things right. If the weekly message ever changes, you can bet the next most-common topic is our need to go out and share the good news of the gospel with others.

This is the third great challenge facing followers of Jesus today: we have a limited view of God's grace. The grace of God, a reality greater than the human intellect can gasp and more accessible than the air we breathe has been captured and domesticated for weekly use. The grace of God, capable of reaching across every culture, every gender, and every generation, has been reduced to mean simply forgiveness for everyone. We have turned it to our uses instead of his.

### Limited Grace, Limited Life:

To those of us who have been in church for some time, grace means that Christians have gotten a great deal. In church circles, grace has variously been defined as "not getting what we deserve," or "God's unmerited favor," or the acronym "God's Riches At Christ's Expense." All of these ideas about grace are true, but tell only part of the truth. This part-truth can actually harm our spiritual formation.

*So I tried another doctor. While I was in the waiting room I overheard this conversation, coming from just beyond the door:*

*"Believe me," said the doctor to an unseen patient. "You're sick, and you're going to die without the cure."*

*"I don't feel sick."*

*"And you won't. Right up 'til when you die."*

*It went on like this for twenty minutes. The doctor finally wore the patient down, and the patient took the medicine.*

*But something strange happened: when he took the medicine, the patient became convinced he **was** sick. He took the medicine because that's what sick people do. It became is new identity. Immediately the doctor tried to tell him the medicine had worked.*

*"OK, then," he said. "All finished. Off you go. You're healed."*

*"But you told me I was sick."*

*"Yes. You were, but now you're healed."*

*"I'm pretty sure I'm sick. You said I would die without the cure."*

*"And so you would have. But you took the cure. It did its work. You're all better. In fact, you're better than better: you're completely new."*

*The two of them argued for a while because the patient was now convinced he was deep-down sick. He left the office, convinced of his illness. It has been his song ever since:*

*"I'm sick and I've taken the cure. I'll always be sick and I'll always take the cure, because that's what sick people do."*

I made that up, too. Or did I? Because I've overheard people who have taken the cure, and they still talk like they're sick. Perhaps you've heard them.

"I'm just a sinner saved by grace," they say (or sing). "There's nothing good inside of me, I'll always be a sinner, because that's what I always do." I've known people who have sung the same song for 40 years. When they agreed with the sin-diagnosis, they apparently thought it described a permanent condition. I know one guy who has memorized Jeremiah 17:9, "The heart is deceitful above all things and beyond cure. Who can understand it?" He apparently made it the signature theme of his walk with God. But shouldn't the cure include a heart transplant?

Dr. Dallas Willard, that great surgeon of the heart, agrees. He warns us against the idea "that the low level of spiritual living among professing Christians is to be regarded as 'only natural,' only what is to be expected." Willard points out our belief--that our destiny is constant failure and Christ's ministry is nothing but unending forgiveness. Many believers have experienced the new birth and are convinced their cosmic state is forever a babe.

We have over-talked about what sin takes away and under-talked about what the Spirit has put in us. Dr. Willard is concerned with more than the cure. True, our life with God must start with the cure, but the possibilities of new life in Christ are--quite literally--endless.

## My Favorite Old Testament Priest

I have a friend who ends every prayer with, "Forgive us for the many ways we've failed you. In Your name we pray, Amen." It doesn't matter if he's blessing the food before a meal or asking for wisdom in an important decision. The closing is his default phrase, like a customized signature at the end of every email.

I'm sure he's sincere--every time he prays it. I wonder if Jesus ever gets tired of hearing it. No friendship on earth could survive if one partner constantly affirmed, "I'm no good." What kind of relationship requires a constant--*constant*--rehashing of our inadequacy? I'd like to suggest an answer: an Old Testament relationship.

The book of Hebrews discusses the practice of forgiveness before Jesus came:

The law is only a shadow of the good things that are coming—not the realities themselves. For this reason it can never, by the same sacrifices repeated endlessly year after year, make perfect those who draw near to worship. Otherwise, would they not have stopped being offered? For the worshipers would have been cleansed once for all, and would no longer have felt guilty for their sins. *But those sacrifices are an annual reminder of sins*. (Hebrews 10: 1-3, my emphasis)

Note the final phrase: the people of Old Testament experienced an annual reminder of their sins. My friend reminds himself of his sin every time he prays. The unspoken message is that he was powerless against sin before he came to Jesus and he is apparently powerless against it after he received Christ.

Willard refers to this as *miserable sinner theology*. Simply put, if we are told often enough that we are miserable sinners who are unable to overcome our shortcomings in God's eyes, sooner or later we will begin to see ourselves in that light—even though we have turned to Christ! For such people "following" Jesus does not include the possibility of being formed into his likeness.

It's not just a problem with our understanding of grace, it's also our understanding of Jesus: his message, his sacrifice, his Kingdom and his mission for us. To see the work of Jesus as nothing but an endless offering for sin is to consign him to the Old Testament priesthood.

Surely his *is* a greater priesthood, capable of altering us at the very core. I'm grateful that he paid the price for my sin--eternally grateful. I am also grateful for his resurrection empowerment, which is capable of changing me from the inside out. Perhaps we can usher Jesus out of the Temple once and for all, and receive him not only as the source of forgiveness, but also the Master teacher of life.

Make no mistake: sin is cancer, and it will kill us in this life and the next. It's serious business, so the Father has provided a serious remedy. It's called the *new birth.* Paul calls it the *new creation,* Peter calls us *new-born babes.* We must determine whether these phrases are merely religious metaphors or if they depict a spiritual reality. The image of spiritual birth also contains the hope of spiritual growth. Are we forever trapped within the cancer of sin?

There's a cure, not just a treatment. Our challenge is how we see Jesus, and for many of us, he is only a treatment. When we limit the work of Jesus to nothing but forgiveness, we lose sight of the possibilities of experiencing a new kind life with him here and now. That would be a shame, because the cure really does work: not only in the next life but in this one as well.

## Where Does Grace Grow?

The 1986 film *The Mission* presented a compelling picture of grace as forgiveness. Robert De Niro played the role of Rodrigo Mendoza, an 18th-century slave trader in

South America. Remorseless and cruel, Mendoza kills his brother in a jealous rage and finds himself imprisoned not only by the authorities, but also by his own relentless guilt. He is embraced by a Jesuit priest (Jeremy Irons), who offers an opportunity to work with the very indigenous people Mendoza had formerly enslaved. As they travel through the Amazon basin Mendoza insists on carrying his former armor in a pack, which he drags behind him—a reminder of his past sins. In an emotional scene midway through the film, a tribesman cuts the pack away as Mendoza struggles to climb a treacherous waterfall. The pack falls away, and Mendoza weeps as he is finally released from his guilt. Christians hailed the movie as a beautiful representation of God's forgiveness and grace.

What many Christians failed to notice was that the act of forgiveness was only the beginning. Mendoza lived among the people he had formerly enslaved and learned to live in peace, both outwardly and inwardly. Whereas in the past he had been driven by blood-lust, he began to embrace the rhythms of an everyday peaceful life. He found rest for his soul in the sacraments administered by the church. These images of Mendoza embracing a new life were also pictures of God's grace in operation. If any Christian reviewer commented upon them, I am unaware. By the end of the film, the depth of his new life was tested when "civilization" intruded upon the village settlement. Whether the grace of God had found its way completely into Mendoza's life I'll leave for the viewer to discover.

The more I read the New Testament, the more all-encompassing grace becomes. Instead of presenting grace as a repeatable sin-cleansing bargain, the Bible presents a grace that continues to reach into our lives day after day in more ways than we expect. The Apostle Paul, under the inspiration of the Holy Spirit, wrote to a young pastor:

The grace of God that brings salvation has appeared to all men. It teaches us to say "No" to ungodliness and worldly passions, and to live self-controlled, upright and godly lives in this present age, while we wait for the blessed hope - the glorious appearing of our great God and Savior, Jesus Christ, who gave himself for us to redeem us from all wickedness and to purify for himself a people that are his very own, eager to do what is good. (Titus 2: 11–14).

Many believers have never heard these verses declared from the pulpit. Grace appears in the passage with phrases like "self-controlled" or "upright and godly lives." What kind of grace is this? If grace means getting off scot-free, why is grace appearing and teaching a new way to live? Most believers are very familiar with "the grace that brings salvation," but not many church-goers have ever heard of a grace that "teaches us to say *No* to ungodliness and worldly passions, and to live self-controlled, upright and godly lives in this present age." Most believers are familiar with a saving grace capable of securing heaven after we die, but have never considered the possibility that God's grace can nurture us in this present age.

Apparently God's grace is after more than wiping the slate clean week after week. The grace of God wants to teach us a new way to live.

## What Does Grace Grow?

"God loves me just the way I am." We are comfortable with that statement; we are less comfortable with, "God loves me so much he won't let me stay just the way I am." First his grace saves, then it teaches. We are OK with receiving forgiveness but perhaps skip school when it comes time to learn how to deny ungodliness and worldly passions, and to live sensible and upright lives. Christians can be forgiven if they are confused at this point: week after we week they are told of the complete work of Jesus on the cross, they are told that there is nothing they can do to earn God's approval or salvation. Yet they are also encouraged to live holy lives and keep the commandments, to walk in a manner that pleases

God. In most pulpits there is a disconnect between the good news of Jesus' sacrifice and our calling to become the light of the world.

Richard Foster, a man who has spent his adult life encouraging Christians to grow in the grace of God, points out that the message of grace is something more than merely a means for gaining forgiveness. Hearing the same message week after week, along with the same remedy, they remain in the same place. "Having been saved by grace," Foster writes, "these people have been paralyzed by it."

The substance of most evangelical preaching is *sin management* (Willard again) by which Christians find forgiveness apart from the call to come and follow. Since this is all they hear, their expectation of the Christian life is a cycle of sin, forgiveness, and more sin. Perhaps most dangerously, the presence of sin is considered "normal" in the life of a believer. Forgiveness is God's antidote. But what if forgiveness is not the antidote but only the emergency triage? What if there was a cure, a real cure that could go deeper and turn us into the kind of creatures for whom sin is *ab*normal? So many people consider any real attempt at imitating Jesus presumption upon God's grace because we cannot save ourselves through "works." Willard explains that

God's grace is not opposed to *effort*, but it is opposed to *earning*. Two pretty different things, aren't they?

This difficulty with grace is the result of decades of emphasis upon his divinity apart from his humanity. Our modern, limited view of grace is directly attributable to the separation we see between Jesus and us. We have been schooled regarding his divinity but the lessons stop at his humanity. Although we may never give voice to the idea, we see Jesus cruising through the challenges of everyday life with the same ease as walking on water. Does your view of Jesus include him as a grace-consumer as well as a grace dispenser?

In liturgical churches the act of receiving the Eucharist is the cleansing moment week by week. Parishioners leave the church in a state of grace fully expecting to fall from that state in the coming days. In evangelical churches the "salvation message" is the staple of preaching week-by-week, coupled with an invitation for believers to come clean with Jesus again and start the week off having received a fresh dose of grace. Whether the grace is administered via the sacrament or through preaching the call to discipleship is not considered a part of that grace. If Christians limit God's grace to mean exclusively the forgiveness of sin, they are locked into immaturity.

If we remain camped at the notion that God's grace is merely another way to describe forgiveness we will never discover that there is grace for everyday living, relationships and ministry to others. In the New Testament alone there are connections between grace and truth, grace and power, grace and spiritual gifts, grace and thanksgiving, grace and generosity, grace and provision, grace and suffering, grace and destiny—and this list is not complete!

Perhaps we are able to recognize the human side of Jesus in the garden of Gethsemane, where he cries out in anguish because of the task ahead. We understand the fear of suffering and the desire to avoid it. We *do* understand why Jesus would say, "Father take this cup from me…" but we have no idea how the grace of God helped Jesus to develop into the kind of person who was also able to pray, "… yet not my will, but yours be done."

If our view of grace is limited to receiving forgiveness, Jesus cannot be our model for how to receive grace, live in grace, and depend upon grace. Who taught Peter, John, Paul and countless other believers how to live the kind of grace-filled life we see in Acts and the history of the church? How does grace apply to everyday life in a manner that we are conscious of the supply and know how to use it?

The gospels display grace in operation when Jesus was tempted in the wilderness, when he wept at the tomb of Lazarus, even when he drove the merchants from the Temple. He is our model for the operation of grace in times of testing, in sorrow, and in every human emotion we face. He can be the author of such grace toward us, because what he has received he freely shares.

### Christian Fatalism:

For years my wife was the director of a crisis pregnancy center in our town. She comforted and held women of nearly all ages as they faced unexpected news, or had nowhere to turn when everyone had walked out on them. One of the most memorable moments my wife experienced was when a teenage girl, a Christian, received the news that her pregnancy test was positive. The young girl's world was undone. She cried in my wife's arms and asked, "How could God let this happen to me?" There on the couch was not the right moment to chide the girl about the sum of her personal choices. She needed comfort. But during the ensuing months, through Bible studies and parenting classes the young woman learned that the freedoms given to us by the Creator are also accompanied by the results of our choices. God respects us so much that he allows the choices we make to have meaning.

Finally the months came to term and a beautiful new life entered the world. The teenage mother returned to my wife's office to show off her trophy of new life, a baby fearfully and wonderfully knit by God. This time the excited young mother declared, "You see, everything happens for a reason!" The beginning of her pregnancy had been met with recriminations against God. The birth of her child was met with a joyful ignorance about the gentle ways of the Father.

"Everything happens for a reason." Perhaps you've heard that before. Perhaps you've said it. I'd like to suggest that there's a world of difference between "Everything happens for a reason," and "God gives reason to everything that happens." The first is Christian superstition; the second declares the glory of God.

The idea that God is somehow pulling the levelers behind the screen of life is what I call Christian fatalism: God is all-powerful. His will cannot be denied. Therefore everything that happens must have been part of his plan from the beginning. He was behind everything all along. Isn't God great?

It's true: God does manage to draw wonderful outcomes from the foolishness of men. It is also true that the glory of

God's power and wisdom is frequently on display in human affairs *in spite* of our choices, not *because* of them. Part of the glory of God is his ability to accomplish his will in the midst of the complexity of a billion human choices. He does not *over-rule* our lives. He works *within* them. He is forgiving, patient, and kind. He knows our weaknesses and chooses to partner with us anyway. What some mean for evil, God turns into good. But he is never the author of that evil.

**The twin dangers of Christian fatalism** are that believers—who ought to be disciples—first come to believe that their sinful choices have been the will of God all along, and second, believers are tempted to believe that whatever happens in life must be ordained by God.

**The first danger** strips away responsibility for our choices and undermines the call of God to repentance as a way of life. Repentance is not simply the doorway into life with God; it is the hallway as well. The New Testament word for repentance is *metanoia,* which means simply to change one's mind, or even better, to re-think our way of life. This rethinking should be an on-going way of life. The Apostle Paul tells us "be transformed by the renewing of your mind" (Romans 12:2). Renewal comes from a continual re-thinking every aspect of life. First God forgives us at the beginning of our relationship, then he teaches us a new way to live.

**The second danger** of Christian fatalism is that believers accept each event in life as part of God's foreordained plan. I have watched followers of Jesus embrace tragedy as if it was sent from God. Sickness is a prime example. Many of God's children embrace sickness as part of God's dealings in their lives. I have heard some Christians refer to cancer as "my gift from God" because they have learned so much through the ordeal of treatment. The clear revelation of scripture is that God is holy and good. He is the Father of lights, the giver of every good and perfect gift. Testing and failure do not come from him. He is not the source of sickness and disease. It's true that in our sickness we can experience the grace of God, or develop Christian virtues such as long-suffering. But that is something very different from ascribing the source of our illness to the heavenly Father. What earthly parent would infect a child with disease in order to teach character lessons? Why would the perfect heavenly Father do what is unthinkable among us?

Sin and sorrow have been loosed on the earth from the very days of the Garden of Eden. We may at times be subject to them, but our Father has never inflicted them upon us for our good. Christian fatalism lures us into a false expression of God's sovereignty and separates from his glory. Perhaps we can discover more his greatness by standing with him against the sin and sorrow of our age.

# Chapter Four
## The Fellowship of Low Expectations

Heinrich Heine lay on his deathbed in 1856. The German poet called his bed "the mattress grave" because he had been confined there for eight years. Born Jewish and converted to Christianity, he lived in Paris with his wife and mistress. There, on a cold February night, he spoke his last words: "Of course God will forgive me, it's his job."

Sometimes I just want forgiveness. I want to be sure I won't be hit by a lightning bolt. I want assurance there is a way out of the mess I've made. I want a system I can depend on, one that guarantees the outcome: forgiven.

I can find the Bible passage I need: "If we confess our sins, he is faithful and just and will forgive us our sins and send us away with the feeling that he has done his job." (1 John 1:9, *well--kind of*) We want a God who is in the forgiveness business the way WalMart is in the cheap junk business: always open, ubiquitous, and always the low price. Always. We want the Jerusalem Temple system of sacrifice, except with as many locations as Starbucks, or more.

In the previous chapter we described the Lord Jesus, trapped in an Old Testament-type priesthood. The book of Hebrews describes the Old Testament system of sacrifice for sin. Hebrews explains there was a High Priest who represented all the people of Israel. Once a year this priest performed his duties and gained forgiveness for all the people--for one more year. The next year he would do it again. And again. The High Priest followed the Old Testament instructions to the letter, and the people of the nation found them selves forgiven. Again. And again. The Old Testament system provided atonement but was incapable of changing the heart.

I like to try to imagine the High Priest sitting down with the people one-on-one after the annual ritual of sacrifice:

"Look," the High Priest asks the busy Jerusalem businessman. "Aren't you tired of doing the same thing every year? Don't you ever want to learn how to live a better life? To grow so close to God that we don't have to do this again and again?"

"Not really," answers the man. "I'm a sinner. It's what I do. You're the Priest--you cleanse me--it's what you do. Why don't we both just do our jobs? See you next year."

I suspect many Christians see Jesus as a WalMart version of the High Priest. We've found a Savior who forgives and forgives, and forgives again. It's true: in Jesus there are springs of forgiveness without end. But there's more. If we want more. There's relationship, empowerment, wisdom, insight, guidance, and strength to break the pattern of sin-and-forgiveness, sin-and-forgiveness.

But Jesus is of a greater priesthood, capable of altering us at the very core. Hebrews tells us that Jesus wasn't even an Old Testament priest in the sense of those who worked at the Temple. Hebrews points us to the shadowy figure named Melchidedek, from the book of Genesis:

This Melchizedek was king of Salem and priest of God Most High. He met Abraham returning from the defeat of the kings and blessed him, and Abraham gave him a tenth of everything. First, the name Melchizedek means "king of righteousness"; then also, "king of Salem" means "king of peace." Without father or mother, without genealogy, without beginning of days or end of life, resembling the Son of God, he remains a priest forever. (Hebrews 7:1-3)

This means Jesus offers something more than forgiveness. He offers *right relationship* and *peace* as well. In part, the message of Hebrews is about finding a way to break the sin-and-forgiveness cycle. What good is forgiveness if we remain the kind of people who are deeply broken in the center of our being? Who needs a priest who fixes up the outside of a person without repairing the inside? All the while Jesus stands ready to make us a new creation. He is the kind of priest who wants to work from the inside out. He's the best kind of Savior, the kind who can transform us from habitual sinners into sons and daughters of the Most High.

Even the Old Testament prophets tried again and again to warn the people of Israel not to trust in religious formulas or systems. They pointed to a personal God who wanted children of his own.

I will give you a new heart and put a new spirit in you; (Ezekiel 36:26)

"I will put my law in their minds and write it on their hearts. I will be their God, and they will be my people. (Jeremiah 31:33)

Wait! There are too many examples to cite. You can trust me on this.

Over and over the prophets urged the people of Israel not to turn their relationship with God into a transaction. They cried out on God's behalf, "I want relationship, not ritual."

The powerful inclination of humanity, however, is to reduce the offer of new birth, new creation, new life and new relationship into nothing more than, "you do your job, and I'll do mine." How many of us do the same with Jesus? It's the difference between getting what we want out of him, or whether he gets what he wants from us--a loving relationship built to last forever.

### I'm Pretty Sure Moses Got This Wrong, Aren't You?

It's amazing how many Christians think the central message of the Old Testament is: *We are a bunch of losers, all of us. Adam and Eve screwed up, and we've been screwing up ever since.* I've been hearing that message since I first turned to Jesus: no one can live up to the laws of God.

Then along came Moses, who totally wrecked my received theology. In his farewell message, after forty years of leading the stiff-necked, rebellious people of Israel desert circles for almost forty years, Moses rallies his countrymen together and says:

For this commandment that I command you today is not too hard for you, neither is it far off. It is not in heaven, that you should say, 'Who will ascend to heaven for us and bring it to us, that we may hear it and do it?' Neither is it beyond the sea, that you should say, 'Who will go over the sea for us and bring it to us, that we may hear it and do it?' But the word is very near you. It is in your mouth and in your heart, so that you can do it. (Deuteronomy 30:11-14)

Poor Moses. It really was time for him to pack it in: he actually believed this group of former Egyptian slaves was capable of living up to the Law of God.

If anyone had proof that people could *not* live up to God's standard, it was Moses. As he spoke these words he stood before the second generation of those who had been set free from slavery--the first generation had turned their backs on Yahweh just weeks after the most spectacular fireworks display in military history. The first generation made a golden calf and worshipped it simply because Moses was a few days late for an appointment.

Forty years later Moses assembled this second generation and said, "You can do this! It's within your reach! Reach into your heart and speak confident words--you can follow the laws you've been given and establish an outpost of heaven on earth." We know how that turned out: the second generation were just as big of losers as the first. And so third generation, and so the next, and on and on.

But here is my question: didn't Moses speak the word of God? Isn't Deuteronomy 30 part of the Bible--that trustworthy, reliable communication from the Creator of the Universe? You see, it wasn't just Moses who thought God's people could hear and do God's will: God himself was speaking through Moses to the people of Israel--and to us--*"you can do this!"*

In fact, God came near to his creation and repeated the message again, this time with a Perfect Messenger:

Do not think that I have come to abolish the Law or the Prophets; I have not come to abolish them but to fulfill them. For truly, I say to you, until heaven and earth pass away, not an iota, not a dot, will pass from the Law until all is accomplished. Therefore whoever relaxes one of the least of these commandments and teaches others to do the same will be called least in the kingdom of heaven, but whoever does them and teaches them will be called great in the kingdom of heaven. For I tell you, unless your righteousness exceeds that of the scribes and Pharisees, you will never enter the kingdom of heaven. ~ Jesus, speaking in Matthew 5:17-20

It seems to me Jesus repeated the message of Deuteronomy. Where Moses failed to provide a perfect example of walking out God's instructions, Jesus himself provided the perfect example. He encouraged us to walk in this manner, and (amazingly) to teach others to do the same. How do the words of Jesus and Moses fit into our understanding of walking with God?

What if, somehow, we could become some kind of new creation capable of bearing fruit that tasted like love, joy, peace, patience, kindness, goodness, faithfulness, gentleness, and self-control? What if? What if obedience to God's good way of life was possible?

**Fellowship of Low Expectations:**

Across the spectrum of Christian worship, our churches are filled with individuals who do not believe Christlikeness is possible. Individual believers have camped beside the river of God's grace so they might drink daily of his forgiveness, unaware that this same grace can can provide spiritual transformation into Christlikeness. Discipleship, they suppose, is for those few super-saints called into the ministry.

Perhaps even more striking is the number of *church leaders* who have largely abandoned the task of making disciples. Our difficulties with discipleship occur not only at the individual level, but also at the level of Christian leadership. The pastoral role in North America is seldom described in terms of reproducing the character and power of Jesus in the people of their congregations. The people of the church do not expect their pastors to be spiritual mentors, and sadly, many pastors do not think the image of Christ is reproducible in their charges. As a result, leadership in Christian churches looks less and less like the Biblical model and more and more like models drawn from the secular world.

Individual Christians struggle in their relationship with Jesus, the impossible mentor. So do pastors. If pastors do not have a realistic expectation that each Christian can live up to the example of Jesus, pastoral ministry becomes about something other than making disciples. If pastors are not convinced of the Christlike destiny of each person in their charge, the role of Christian leadership drifts away from the Biblical example toward any number of earth-bound substitutes. These earth-bound substitutes may each be morally good in their own right, but they will miss the high calling of developing a royal priesthood capable of demonstrating the glory of God to a watching world.

How many pastors carry the vision Peter expressed for the people in his charge:

But you are a chosen people, a royal priesthood, a holy nation, a people belonging to God, that you may declare the praises of him who called you out of darkness into his wonderful light. Once you were not a people, but now you are the people of God; once you had not received mercy, but now you have received mercy. Dear friends, I urge you, as aliens and strangers in the world, to abstain from sinful desires, which war against your soul. Live such good lives among the pagans that, though they accuse you of doing wrong, they may see your good deeds and glorify God on the day he visits us. (I Peter 2:9-12)

These four verses express high expectations for the assembled people of God. Consider this partial list drawn exclusively from these four verses: God's people possess a calling for ministry; God's people possess a godly legacy of royalty; they are ordained to represent God; they are the light-bearers for the world; God's people have a new identity with one another; and God's people have a reason to embrace life-change. Pastor Peter presents a vision where the conduct of average Christians will elicit praise for God from those who are not yet believers. Modern pastors rarely present such a high view of those they are called to shepherd.

In the first years of my work as a pastor I attended a weekly breakfast "prayer meeting" of local pastors. I was looking for practical help in fulfilling my vision of equipping every believer to do the work of the ministry. Assembled were church leaders from a variety of faith traditions, both liturgical and Evangelical, representing a variety of the

American denominational spectrum. In two years of regular meetings with these shepherds of the flock, the only subject which drew complete agreement was their low opinion of the people they were called to lead. Each pastor shared story after story of petty arguments and disagreements, all to the same point: the people were impossible to lead! Clearly, I had fallen in with the wrong crowd. It will come as no surprise that by the time I celebrated my fifth year in the pastorate, every single pastor who attended the prayer breakfast had moved on to other churches or left the ministry.

If pastors do not have high expectations of those in their care, the door swings both ways. Local churches place any number of expectations on their pastors: preaching, visiting the sick, counseling, and supervising the ministries of the church are all standard aspects of the job description. Reproducing the character and power of Jesus in the lives of individual members is not often on the list. Since most Christians do not consider themselves capable of Christlikeness, they do not look to their pastor for assistance in spiritual formation. Indeed, any pastor bold enough to declare, "You-all bear little resemblance to Jesus, so I am here to re-shape your lives," will likely face opposition from the congregation. They hired him to perform religious services, not change their lives!

The pastoral challenge of our day is reflected in the mutual low expectations between shepherd and sheep. The issue is more than education, it is priorities of ministry. In some church circles, there is a common saying from the pulpit: "There are only two questions God will ask when you get to heaven: 'Do you know my Son?' and, 'How many other people did you bring with you?'" These questions reflect the priorities of many evangelical pastors. Evangelical churches have placed leading others to the conversion experience as the highest calling of the church.

Liturgical churches have frequently placed corporate social action as the highest calling of the church. Their witness is to the local community through the corporate actions of the congregation. While taking the lead in ministry to the poor or in matters of social justice, the formation of disciples capable of reflecting the character and power of Jesus is left behind. The emphasis is on the prophetic voice of the church to a dying world.

In both evangelical and liturgical circles, the growth and maturity of believers is secondary at best. The consequences are plain: we have produced congregations of people willing to work for Jesus, but unable to relate to him.

Pastors may still teach in Bible studies, but the object of Bible study becomes academic knowledge instead of conformity to Christ. Pastors may still organize congregational outreach activities, but the object of these efforts will be church-growth instead of gathering the next generation of disciples. Pastors may encourage their congregations to serve their communities, but the mission of the local church becomes a vague civic good instead of spiritual formation in the lives of their congregants. The deceptive challenge of pastoral ministry apart from making disciples is that nearly *any* activity can benefit the church as an institution without ever fulfilling the mandate of the Great Commission.

No one is the wiser for the loss: since church members have difficulty in grasping the idea that they can be conformed to the image of Christ they settle for the comforting notion that they have at least done something worthwhile. Since pastors do not see the potential of each Christian to become a Christlike disciple they will settle for achievable, measurable corporate goals which may be noble but do not further the Great Commission.

Lack of vision by pastors results in lowered expectations, dumbed-down preaching and a general chaplaincy that considers victorious Christian living a pipe dream. Instead of Biblically-inspired confidence in the "imperishable seed" residing in each believer, pastors' vision for each person in their care is reduced to caring for people who are destined to live in a cycle of failure-and-forgiveness.

We have become the Fellowship of Low Expectations.

## Where Are the Answers?

These first four chapters have outlined what I believe to be the central problem in pursuing life as a disciple of Jesus, the Master of Living.

We see his divinity but not his humanity, so we think it's complete folly to aspire to live up to his example.

We are reluctant to receive help from human mentors because we see so clearly that they do not measure-up to the Lord's example. Although we may give ourselves a pass on imitating the master, we are reluctant to hand out the same pass to our leaders.

We have changed God's definition of grace to suit our own needs, and ignored the life-changing power the grace of God.

We have settled into an un-easy partnership with the leaders of God's people. We will not expect much from them if they will not expect too much of us. Instead of going deep, we simply look to invite others into the Fellowship of Low Expectations.

Any student of Jesus who wants to take discipleship seriously must come to terms with these issues.

I believe there are answers! In Section Two of this book we will look at the outline of these answers. In section three we will do our best to apply them. Are you willing?

# Part Two:
# Five Answers

# CHAPTER FIVE
## HOW DID HE BECOME THE MAN HE WAS?

Away in a manger, no crib for a bed,

The little Lord Jesus laid down his sweet head,

The stars in the sky look down where he lay,

The little Lord Jesus asleep in the hay.

It may not be Christmas time as you read this, but this carol raises an important question to anyone who wants to follow Jesus. The song celebrates the Incarnation, literally, the *enfleshment* of Jesus, when God Himself became man. It is a powerful carol because any parent well remembers the beauty and mystery of their child asleep in the crib. We can relate to sleeping babies. But then…

The cattle are lowing, the poor Baby wakes

The little Lord Jesus, no crying He makes…

Right here--at the words, "no crying he makes" the song departs from our personal experience. Most mothers would begin to worry about a baby that never cries. What kind of baby was this Jesus? Did he ever cry?

Will you indulge me in some foolishness? This baby Jesus, God Incarnate: how did he receive the Magi when they came to worship him? Did the infant in the manger invite them in and gesture for them to sit? Did he say, "Please, come in. You must be exhausted from your journey." Did the newborn baby thank them for their thoughtful gifts? Or imagine Jesus as a young boy learning the family business at his father's side: the sinless Son of God, perhaps six years old, driving a nail into a board for the very first time. Did he hold the hammer correctly? Did he drive the nail straight and true? Or, like all children, did he gain his skill through experience? When the Perfect Human Being first held a saw and cut a piece of wood, did he cut the board correctly? And if he did not, what does this say of his divinity? Was he still perfect?

## The Fight to Defend his Divinity:

Throughout the history of the church, Jesus has been worshipped as God come to earth. Jesus Christ has been rightly extolled and revered as the second person of the

Trinity: God the Son. With the rise of the Enlightenment, however, philosophers and theologians reconsidered their foundations. By the 19$^{th}$ and 20$^{th}$ centuries, the church saw repeated attacks upon the divinity of Christ. In secular academies, and even in some Christian seminaries, the search for the "Authentic Jesus" produced an outpouring of work that indicated Jesus was a "only a man." By the second half of the 20$^{th}$ century, debate over the identity of Jesus reached fever pitch. In 1966 Time Magazine popularized Nietzsche's century-old phrase "God is Dead," and predicted a coming age of "Christian Atheism" that would embrace the teachings of Jesus without the restraints of supernatural religious belief. In 1977 *The Myth of God Incarnate*, edited by John Hick, drew together controversial essays from Jurgen Moltmann, Walter Kasper, and Wolfhart Pannenberg among others that overthrew traditional theology concerning the Divine person of Jesus Christ. All of these theologians (and more) declared that any notion of the divinity of Jesus Christ was an "overlay" by his followers who penned the scriptural record.

Traditional churches responded to these attacks vigorously, affirming the scriptural witness and theological necessity of Christ's divinity. In the 2,000 years since Jesus' earthly ministry Christians around the world have received him as the God-Man. From Catholic cathedrals to evangelical pulpits, the centuries-old teaching of the church was restated: Jesus Christ is God come to earth. However, this defense came at a cost. For two generations or more now, only half of the divine equation has been emphasized. While fighting off the attacks of those who would try to strip Jesus of his divine nature, church leaders have seldom presented the truth of Christ's humanity. The equally important truth of Christ's humanity was down played, and average believers lost sight of the classic teaching of the church: Jesus Christ is fully God *and* fully man.

During the Christmas season we celebrate the wonder of God coming to earth in a human body, but few of us have taken time to meditate on the significance of the Incarnation. True, we can smile at the foolishness of the baby Jesus playing host to the Magi because no baby has ever come into the world with all the skills necessary to succeed in life. Every child grows and learns. But if Jesus is our example in both behavior and ministry, we should ask, *how did he become the man he was?* The gospels give us barely a glimpse of Jesus until he begins his ministry at age 30. We have the birth narratives in Matthew and Luke: warm-hearted stories of Joseph and Mary; the wonder and beauty of that first Christmas night with angels, shepherds, and a stable; the young family of three fleeing to Egypt in order to escape

King Herod's murderous rage. Between birth and age 30, though, we get only one snapshot of Jesus growing up. Luke's gospel gives us twelve short verses that cover everything between birth and maturity:

> "And the child grew and became strong; he was filled with wisdom, and the grace of God was upon him. Every year his parents went to Jerusalem for the Feast of the Passover. When he was twelve years old, they went up to the Feast, according to the custom. After the Feast was over, while his parents were returning home, the boy Jesus stayed behind in Jerusalem, but they were unaware of it. Thinking he was in their company, they traveled on for a day. Then they began looking for him among their relatives and friends. When they did not find him, they went back to Jerusalem to look for him. After three days they found him in the temple courts, sitting among the teachers, listening to them and asking them questions. Everyone who heard him was amazed at his understanding and his answers. When his parents saw him, they were astonished. His mother said to him, "Son, why have you treated us like this? Your father and I have been anxiously searching for you."
>
> "Why were you searching for me?" he asked. "Didn't

you know I had to be in my Father's house?" But they did not understand what he was saying to them. Then he went down to Nazareth with them and was obedient to them. But his mother treasured all these things in her heart. And Jesus grew in wisdom and stature, and in favor with God and men." (Luke 2:40–52)

This intriguing passage gives us a look at Jesus the twelve year-old boy. What was Jesus doing in the Temple that day? Many people think he was teaching, but the inspired text reveals that he was *listening and asking questions*. His hunger for God had driven him to the one place where he could be sure of God the Father's presence. At twelve years-old, just before his Bar-Mitzvah, Jesus sought answers to his questions. He was about to become a "son of the covenant," to take his place as an adult in the Jewish community. The teachers of the Law were amazed at Jesus. His questions revealed a depth of thought and a sincere desire to know more. Jesus tells Joseph and Mary they should have looked there first, at "my Father's house." I believe the young Jesus went there to ask about God. His questions were so profound the teachers of the Law invited him into the dialogue.

I like to speculate what those questions might have been. Luke tells us Jesus returned to the Temple as a grown man, and stumped the teachers of Israel with a question about the person and identity of the Messiah:

> Then Jesus said to them, "How is it that they say the Christ is the Son of David? David himself declares in the Book of Psalms: "'The Lord said to my Lord: "Sit at my right hand until I make your enemies a footstool for your feet."' David calls him 'Lord.' How then can he be his son?" (Luke 20:41–44)

Could this have been one of the questions that captured the heart of the twelve year-old Jesus? Luke also reminds us that the young Jesus "Grew in wisdom and stature." (Luke 2: 52) Jesus, the God-Man, grew in wisdom and stature. His growth was characteristically human. He acquired his learning in the same way each of us did: babies learn how to speak, children learn how to read and write. Can we imagine Jesus growing in the same manner? To imagine Jesus in this way does no harm to his role as the perfect sacrifice for our sin. The writer of Hebrews extols Jesus as the perfect High Priest while simultaneously reminding his readers of the Lord's humanity:

> During the days of Jesus' life on earth, he offered up prayers and petitions with loud cries and tears to

the one who could save him from death, and he was heard because of his reverent submission. Although he was a son, *he learned obedience* from what he suffered and, once made perfect, he became the source of eternal salvation for all who obey him.
(Hebrews 5:7–9, emphasis added)

How many of us have considered the possibility that Jesus *learned* to obey the Heavenly Father? In this passage from Hebrews we are sometimes tempted to connect "learned obedience" with the suffering mentioned immediately after. "Of course," we think, "Jesus suffered terribly at the cross." But this would miss the point: his life of obedience led him to the cross. This passage mentions the "loud cries and tears," and we immediately connect the phrase with the fateful night Jesus spent at Gethsemane but it's also possible that Hebrews is referring to other moments, when Jesus learned how to lay his desires down before the Father's direction.

### The Only Sober Man in the World:

Even his sinless life became part of his growth and learning. Adapting an image from the church Fathers of the second century, author William P. Sampson offers this parable, comparing Jesus to the only sober person in a world drunk with sin:

He arrives at the office Christmas party rather late.
No one has left yet, and everyone is quite happy now.
He joins a laughing group. There's a childish remark
at which everyone explodes with laughter. Then a
half-word and they laugh again uncontrollably... To
be so clear-headed in the presence of such confusion,
so honest in the midst of such lying, to be so filled
with affection in the midst of such antagonism,
animosity, to be so real in the midst of such
phoniness. His heart is moved to identify with this sad
people. They are his. He belongs to them.

Like the only sober man at a party, he saw reality when
others could not. Jesus embodied a human life lived to it's
full potential. This casts light on the assertion in Hebrews
4:15, "For we do not have a high priest who is unable to
sympathize with our weaknesses, but we have one who has
been tempted in every way, just as we are—yet was without
sin." Rather than separating him from the rest of humanity,
his sinless life enabled him to see more clearly into the
human condition.

This point is important because when we encounter
Jesus as a 30 year-old man his holiness is evident to all who
meet him, and his level of ministry to the masses is
astonishing. His character was unassailable. He taught with

authority. If Jesus modeled ministry for us by healing the sick, casting out demons and raising the dead, by what power did he do these things? If we want to settle for nothing less than the best role-model possible, we need to consider how he became such a man. If Jesus accomplished moral excellence and supernatural ministry exclusively through the privilege of his identity as the Son of God, how can he expect us to follow him? Any serious follower of Jesus should take time to consider—*how did Jesus do the things he did?* Was he sinless because he had some advantage over you or me? Did he heal the sick or multiply the bread and fish because he had some secret power not open to any of his followers? If Jesus did these things because he was the Boss' son, isn't it unfair for him to expect us to become like him?

### Did Jesus Take a Short-Cut?

Luke chapter 4 depicts the very beginning of Jesus' ministry as an adult, the very first sermon recorded in that Gospel. It is short, and revealing:

> He went to Nazareth, where he had been brought up, and on the Sabbath day he went into the synagogue, as was his custom. And he stood up to read. The scroll of the prophet Isaiah was handed to him. Unrolling it, he found the place where it is written:

"The Spirit of the Lord is on me,

because he has anointed me

to preach good news to the poor.

He has sent me to proclaim freedom for the prisoners

and recovery of sight for the blind,

to release the oppressed,

to proclaim the year of the Lord's favor."

Then he rolled up the scroll, gave it back to the

attendant and sat down. The eyes of everyone in the

synagogue were fastened on him, and he began by

saying to them, "Today this scripture is fulfilled in

your hearing." (Luke 4:16-21)

Jesus selected the passage from Isaiah that begins plainly
"The Spirit of the Lord is upon me."

"The Spirit of the Lord is upon me." He didn't pick this
passage randomly, the text tells us he was looking for this
passage. Jesus announced the beginning of his ministry with
words that explained his relationship with the Holy Spirit.
Everything that follows in the life and ministry of Jesus flows
from the operation of the Holy Spirit in his life. In fact, Luke
had already pointed out the role of the Holy Spirit in Jesus'
baptism (3:22) and in the 40 days of testing in the wilderness
(4:1&14). In Luke's second work, the book of Acts, he

quotes the Apostle Peter, who gives a one-sentence summary of the ministry of Jesus:

> "You know what has happened throughout Judea, beginning in Galilee after the baptism that John preached -- *how God anointed Jesus of Nazareth with the Holy Spirit and power*, and how he went around doing good and healing all who were under the power of the devil, because God was with him." (Acts 10:38-39, emphasis added)

Many followers of Jesus have never considered Peter's summary of Jesus' life. Jesus did what he did by the power of the Holy Spirit, not by virtue of his unique identity as the Son of God. Peter concludes his statement not with the phrase "because he was God," but rather "Because God was with him." Make no mistake--Jesus is God Himself come to earth. His example for life and ministry, however, is through the Holy Spirit's empowerment, the same Spirit that's available to his followers. The same Holy Spirit who helped Jesus is available to every believer. If the life of Jesus is truly our example then his character and his works should be the goal of all who follow him.

As the record of his life unfolds in the gospels we are faced with this question: *how did Jesus do the things he did?* We cannot choose to say simply, "he was the Messiah, God come to earth." From the beginning his earliest followers understood that Jesus lived a life that demonstrated full reliance on the Holy Spirit, a life in perfect submission to the Father's will. His life was a model for anyone who would follow him, a model of both moral excellence and ministry guided by the Holy Spirit. How can his life be a model for anyone if his character and power cannot be imitated? Whether we articulate the question or not, each of us must wrestle with the nature of Jesus--was he God or was he man? If he was only a man, how can his death pay the price for all mankind? If he is "only" God, how can he reasonably expect his followers to live up to his example? It is an important wrestling match because our answer may well determine our own progress as a follower of Jesus.

Jesus clearly expected his followers to do the same kind of works he did. How can we explain his statement in John 14:12? "I tell you the truth, anyone who has faith in me will do what I have been doing. He will do even greater things than these, because I am going to the Father." This is a breath-taking statement. "Anyone," he says "will do what I have been doing." Could Jesus mean he wanted his followers to imitate every aspect of his ministry? The instructions he gave to the twelve in Luke 9:2 are clear: "he sent them out to preach the kingdom of God and to heal the sick." Just one chapter later in Luke's gospel, Jesus widened the commission to at least 70 of his followers. In short order they returned joyfully, "Lord, even the demons submit to us in your name." (Luke 10:17) Even as Jesus was pleased with their works he reminded them of their own need for redemption, and then filled with Holy Spirit-inspired joy, made a most startling statement: "I praise you, Father, Lord of heaven and earth, because you have hidden these things from the wise and learned, and revealed them to little children. Yes, Father, for this was your good pleasure."

The "wise and learned" debated the nature of Jesus the man and Jesus the Son of God for nearly 400 years. Finally, in 431AD at the first Council of Ephesus the church settled on this formulation: Jesus was one person, not two separate people: completely God *and* completely man, all wrapped up into one person. Both aspects of his nature are important for everyday living. Only God's own Son can purchase the redemption of all humanity--no human sacrifice will do. Our forgiveness rests completely in the sufficiency of God's own sacrifice. We need to approach him as the only one capable of dispensing divine mercy and grace. At the same time, Jesus is the example of a human life lived in full accordance with the Father's will. His character and kindness flowed from the presence of the Holy Spirit within him. We must see that his miracles were accomplished through the power of the Holy Spirit, not by virtue of some divine standing as the Son of God. When Jesus operated under the direction of the Holy Spirit, he showed us how it is done. That is, he calls us to be like him in every way.

Simple passages like Luke 2:52 (about his childhood) point to the fact that Jesus lived a very human life. Other, more enigmatic verses like Hebrews 5:8 seem to point to the fact that Jesus modeled obedience—an obedience he won by suffering the same difficulties we face. The first five chapters in the book of Hebrews assert that while Jesus is greater than any man in history, he remains human. When the writer of Hebrews quotes Psalm 8 he is pointing out that Jesus was made for a little while "lower than the angels," in order to show how God can be glorified by a man who lives in submission to the will of God. Perhaps most challenging of all are verses like Matthew 10:7-8, which indicate that Jesus had higher expectations for his followers than we have today.

To ignore the humanity of Jesus is to ignore his call to be like him in every respect. To over-emphasize his divinity is to excuse ourselves for living powerless lives, lives powerless over sin or powerless over the sicknesses and demonization so prevalent in our world today. How did he become the man he was? The simple answer is he lived in the presence and the power of the Holy Spirit. The more difficult answer is that he calls us to live the same way.

# Chapter Six
## Jesus, The Firstborn

If you look at the information on my driver's license it will tell you that I'm two inches taller and twenty pounds lighter than I really am--I figured if I get pulled over by a policeman I'll be sitting in the car so he can't really tell I'm lying. At five-foot eight and 180 pounds, I'm hardly a candidate for any professional sport. This has always been a great disappointment to my Dad. By the time I was in first grade my father encouraged me to consider a career as a professional rodeo clown.

"Son," he sighed, "if you're going to live up to your potential, you'd better start wearing funny clothes and dodging wild animals."

Years later, after I flunked out of rodeo clown school, I became a pastor, and later a writer. So much for fulfilling my potential: I should have set my sights lower.

## Jesus, Our True Potential:

If you want to know what your full potential looks like as a Christian, look at Jesus. All that he did during his earthly ministry was done through reliance upon the Holy Spirit and by looking to the Father for direction. In the last chapter we observed that the previous century emphasized the divinity of Christ and his unique role as God's only-begotten Son. Our understanding of his humanity began to fade. Not only did we lose sight of how he became the man he was, we also lost sight of the fullness of his mission on Earth. In part, that mission was to give new life and a new family identity to everyone who trusts in him. That new identity, available right now to anyone who will follow him, is "Child of God."

Jesus is fully God and fully man: we *worship* Jesus because he is God; we can *pattern our lives after him* because in his humanity he lived the perfect human life as our example. We should recognize the difference between his unique sacrificial death on the cross and the pattern of living he set for us during his earthly ministry.

His death on the cross is unique because of who he is—the sinless perfect Son of God, the Lamb of God who takes away the sins of the world. No one else could accomplish what Jesus accomplished on the cross, because his perfect sacrifice came by virtue of his identity as God come to earth. His sacrifice was for the sin of all peoples, in all times, in all places. God's own blood is the only thing that could satisfy the guilt of our sin. His death was unique: one time, once, for all. God himself provided the lamb. No one else could do it and no one else will ever have to do it again. We have emphasized the death and resurrection of Jesus as God's only Son precisely because only God could do it.

There is, however, a danger of over-emphasis: when we concentrate on the substitutionary death of Jesus to the exclusion of his life and teaching we limit his ministry to a divine rescue mission—a rescue mission that only becomes effective for us when we die. When we see his ministry exclusively as the action that purchased heaven for us it's difficult to make the connection between his sacrifice and our everyday lives. Many Christians are moved emotionally by his suffering on the cross. Many are grateful that he paid a debt he did no owe. Many Christians understand that they have no hope of heaven apart from the price Jesus paid on their behalf. But apart from gratitude for his kindness there is little connection between what Jesus did then and how we can live today.

Here is the challenge: our appreciation for what he did does not empower us to fulfill his mission or our potential. Our gratitude for his suffering does release the wisdom, insight, or strength for each one of us to live as a new kind of person. Jesus urged his followers to "Take my yoke upon you and learn from me, for I am gentle and humble in heart, and you will find rest for your souls." (Matthew 11:28-30) The rest he speaks of is not our eternal rest, but rest and peace for everyday living. His gentle strength and humility may have led him to the cross but they are also character traits available to his disciples today. He offers the opportunity for us to learn from him—not about how to go to heaven but about how heaven can come to earth now. This is the very first request we are taught to pray in the Lord's Prayer: "Let Your Kingdom come, let Your will be done *on earth as it is in heaven.*" (Matthew 6:10, emphasis added). During his earthly ministry his wisdom, his actions, the radical nature of the gospel of the Kingdom of God, and his powerful works were examples of how we could live on earth as well.

**Jesus, the Firstborn. Five Distinctives:**

After we recognize how Jesus became the man he was, the next step in our spiritual formation is to see him as "the firstborn." It's important for us to understand this part of Jesus' identity, because the label *firstborn* encompasses both parts of who he is: God and Man.

The New Testament refers to Jesus as the "firstborn" in at least five contexts: as Mary's firstborn child (Luke 2: 7 & 23), as the "first born among many brothers" (Romans 8:29), as the "firstborn over all creation" (Colossians 1: 15), the "firstborn of the dead" (Colossians 1: 18 and Revelation 1:5), and finally as God's firstborn son (Hebrews 1: 6). In the first century the concept of firstborn was well known, both in the natural sense and in a spiritual sense as well. You can find these references to Jesus as the firstborn in the gospels, the letters of Paul, the preaching of Hebrews and the book of Revelation. Rarely do we find one repeated idea spanning so many New Testament genres.

When Jesus was born to Mary he entered the world with a specific Jewish identity—that of a firstborn son. Beginning with the Bible account of Esau and Jacob to the Law of Moses, the firstborn son was special. He was set apart to the Lord Himself (Exodus 13:2). The firstborn was the one who "opened" the womb: after one child was born, there was an expectation that more would follow. This idea that more children will follow the firstborn is also the sense of Paul's passage in Romans. "For those God foreknew he also predestined to be conformed to the likeness of his Son, that he might be the firstborn among many brothers." (Romans 8:29) God intended that after Jesus many more of his brothers would follow. In Colossians Paul also indicates that firstborn means more than birth order, it means the highest place: Jesus is the "firstborn over all creation," that is, nothing in the created realm can equal him. Paul then explores another image immediately by recognizing that just as Jesus conquered death, so could his followers: "And he is the head of the body, the church; he is the beginning and the firstborn from among the dead, so that in everything he might have the supremacy." (Colossians 1:18) This speaks of our resurrection from death. Jesus is revealed as the first born from the dead. In the human imagination it's a ghastly image, but in the Biblical witness the resurrected body of Jesus is beautiful and glorious beyond telling. This glorious resurrected body, we too will receive. Finally, the writer of Hebrews states plainly that Jesus is not only the firstborn of Mary, but of God himself.

What is the impact of these verses when we put them together? We can pull all these ideas together into one statement: *the Father desired to have many children, but his firstborn Son would occupy the highest place by virtue of birth order and by virtue of his supremacy.* Jesus is unique, he has the highest place. No one can or will surpass him. He also makes possible a new creation, a group of people called the children of God. Jesus is the "last Adam," (1 Corinthians 15:45), and Paul calls everyone who follows Jesus a "new creation." (2 Corinthians 5:17) This new creation is effective both now and also in the age to come.

Without actually encountering the phrase firstborn, we find the same idea in the prologue of John's gospel: "He was in the world, and though the world was made through him, the world did not recognize him. He came to that which was his own, but his own did not receive him. Yet to all who received him, to those who believed in his name, he gave the right to become children of God--children born not of natural descent, nor of human decision or a husband's will, but born of God." (John1:10–13) In this prologue John suggests that in Christ God is beginning to break down the division between heaven and Earth. The idea is so important that John's gospel reinforces this theme twice more in the chapter. First, John the Baptist witnesses the opening of the heavens as the Spirit is poured out on Jesus. Second, Jesus promises Nathanael that he will see the heavens opened and the angels ascending and descending. In both cases the resources of heaven are beginning to break through from the heavenly realm into the earthly realm. Together these three images prepare us to encounter Jesus' careful use of words when he talks with Nicodemus.

John's gospel is famous for the encounter between Jesus and Nicodemus in chapter three. Evangelicalism has drawn the phrase "born again" from this chapter, which details a discussion between a teacher in Israel and the Lord himself. Jesus told Nicodemus that the born again experience was necessary to see the Kingdom of God (John 3:3). A more literal rendering of the phrase "born again" is actually *born from above*. Nicodemus understood Jesus' meaning in terms of a second birth, as the context shows, but the author of the fourth gospel, under the inspiration of the Holy Spirit chose his words carefully: while affirming the need for a spiritual rebirth, the words *"born from above"* point to the source of that birth—it comes from above. It comes from heaven. This was true of Jesus, who came from heaven to earth, and it is true of those who follow him. The source of the new birth is from above.

Jesus, the firstborn among many, has opened the womb of heaven. Now everyone who is born from above has the resources of heaven available. The nature and the power of the resurrection dwell in each new child of God. This is no mere formality: the reality is that because the womb of heaven has been opened by Jesus, the firstborn, each believer has the potential to bring heaven to earth. Through the new birth we possess our heavenly citizenship—not a citizenship that comes in handy when we die, but a citizenship that can change the way we think and act now. Jesus is the firstborn of a new race. Firstborn means the pattern has been set. It means others will follow. Those who are *born from above* receive heaven's DNA in them here, now.

### When Does Eternal Life Begin?

If our view of the new birth in Jesus Christ is limited to going to heaven when we die, then the power of being born again is only effective when we die. If, however, we understand our new birth as being *born from above*, it means that heaven is breaking into earth in each new child of God. The presence of the Holy Spirit that empowered Jesus and the resurrection power of that Spirit are available to each new child of God right away. Another possible way to understand this is to ask the question, *when* does eternal life begin: when we die, or when we are born from above? Sadly, too many believers define eternal life as "Going to heaven when we die," instead of heaven coming to earth at the moment we are born into the family of God. Jesus offered a definition of eternal life in John's gospel. It had nothing to do with going to heaven after our death, and everything to do with becoming alive to the Father. "Now this is eternal life: that they may know you, the only true God, and Jesus Christ, whom you have sent." (John 17:3) When do we begin to know God? After we die and go to heaven? To be sure, we will know him better when that happens, but the relationship begins as soon as we turn to him.

Our ability to see Jesus as the firstborn is more than a Bible-study lesson. Once we see him in this light, our role as children of God takes on new meaning, new possibilities, and new responsibilities. He opened the way for us to continue his Kingdom mission. Heaven's resources pour into us. Jesus relied upon the Holy Spirit to walk in obedience, and he sent the Holy Spirit to help us do the same. He relied upon the Holy Spirit to do powerful works that authenticated his message, and he sent the Holy Spirit to do the same for us. This idea is not Pentecostalism in any traditional or cultural sense. It is recognizing that while Jesus indeed came to save us from our sins, he also came to empower us to live Godly lives that can look substantially like his life. It is recognizing that his mission not only included securing the "sweet by-and-by" of Heaven but also equipping us in the "nasty now-and-now" of living on Earth. It calls us to live the kind of lives that demonstrate by our example that he is able to save, even right now.

The decision to receive Jesus as Lord and Savior includes the promise of Heaven, of course. It also includes a miraculous transformation to become part of God's family. Just as Jesus commissioned his original followers to proclaim that the Kingdom of God is breaking in, so he commissions us to present the same message, and to demonstrate the message in the same ways. He does not entrust this task to servants, he gives it to family. What begins as a master-disciple relationship in the gospels morphs into one between friends, and after his ascension, the relationship is described as family: "the one who makes men holy and those who are made holy are of the same family. So Jesus is not ashamed to call them brothers." (Hebrews 2:11) The call to come and follow is actually a call to join the family business. Not as a hired hand, but as a child of God.

### The Firstborn Produces The Firstfruit:

If Jesus is the firstborn, we are firstfruit. James describes the followers of Jesus this way: "He chose to give us birth through the word of truth, that we might be a kind of firstfruits of all he created." (James 1:18) The Biblical notion of the firstfruits is the choice portion of the crop, and a harbinger of what the rest of the harvest will look like. Jesus was the good seed that was sown: that seed fell into the Earth and died. Just as he described, that seed did not abide alone, but instead bore much fruit. Part of his purpose was the fruit of his life would be reproduced in those who came after him. This fruit, his followers, would look and "taste" like Jesus in both his character and his works.

Jesus said he is the one who makes all things new (Revelation 21:5): a new earth, a new heaven, and a new people drawn from every people group on the earth. The fulfillment of these words surely comes at the end of this age, but right now, in this present age, Jesus planted evidence of what the age to come will look like. What will this new age look like? What kind of people has Jesus planted? According to the Apostle Peter, we *are* that people right now! He reveals how the first followers of Jesus saw themselves: "But you are a chosen people, a royal priesthood, a holy nation, a people belonging to God, that you may declare the praises of him who called you out of darkness into his wonderful light. Once you were not a people, but now you are the people of God; once you had not received mercy, but now you have received mercy." (1 Peter 2:9-10)

The early church believed that Jesus had opened the way for heaven to invade Earth. This invasion meant that

everyone who followed Jesus could draw on the same
resources that Jesus used. Our lives should reflect the
promise of Heaven. The expectation of the early church was
that because Jesus had opened the way, Heaven would
regularly break into the everyday business of Earth. Consider
the prayer of the early church in Jerusalem:

> When they heard this, they raised their voices
> together in prayer to God. "Sovereign Lord," they
> said, "you made the heaven and the earth and the sea,
> and everything in them. You spoke by the Holy Spirit
> through the mouth of your servant, our father David:
> " 'Why do the nations rage
> and the peoples plot in vain?
> The kings of the earth take their stand
> and the rulers gather together
> against the Lord
> and against his Anointed One.
> Indeed Herod and Pontius Pilate met together with the
> Gentiles and the people of Israel in this city to
> conspire against your holy servant Jesus, whom you
> anointed. They did what your power and will had
> decided beforehand should happen. Now, Lord,
> consider their threats and enable your servants to
> speak your word with great boldness. Stretch out your

hand to heal and perform miraculous signs and wonders through the name of your holy servant Jesus."

After they prayed, the place where they were meeting was shaken. And they were all filled with the Holy Spirit and spoke the word of God boldly. (Acts 4:24–31)

Notice the relationship between the people of God and the work of God: his people would speak boldly, and God would heal and perform miraculous signs and wonders through them. This was the pattern set by Jesus in the gospels, and it was the pattern applied to the church in Acts. Jesus was the firstborn of Heaven; the church was the firstfruit of his ministry. The early church was both the harvest and the example of the whole harvest would look like. This was true then, and it is true now. The complete harvest comes at the end of the age. Meanwhile the church exhibits the promise of that harvest.

It's a glorious picture of the church, but sadly, a picture largely obscured by our current condition today. Perhaps we can dare to hope that the church will someday rise to this calling, but the immediate challenge is to see that the church is comprised of individual family members. The *we* begins with Christ formed in *me*.

# CHAPTER SEVEN
## UNTIL CHRIST IS FORMED IN YOU

I spent 10 years of my life living in Ft. Worth, Texas and working as a truly mediocre salesman. It's a wonder I earned enough money to pay the bills. Sometimes I didn't. I once attended a sales seminar where I learned that sales was a *numbers game.* The business-savvy masters of the seminar explained, "If you see enough people, you'll make your quota every month."

When I returned to work I bragged to my boss that I would spend the next day cold-calling for prospects. I headed out of the office into the Texas summer determined to make the numbers work for me. At the end of the day I returned a defeated man.

"I made 58 cold-calls today, but I didn't get a single sale."

"I suppose you could've made 59 calls," he answered. "But someone probably slowed you down by asking a question about your product."

His answer was a revelation. Although he was talking about business, I saw the difference between two kingdoms: worldly wisdom is obsessed with numbers, but God's kingdom depends upon eternal qualities like listening, trust, and relationship.

### Growth, Not Numbers:

In the last 150 years much of the North American church has had an obsession with numbers. We count decisions for Christ. We keep track of average weekend attendance at our church. We certainly count the money in the offering. Like that mediocre salesman, God forbid anyone slow us down with a question. It's not always been that way: as far as I know, the greatest evangelist in the New Testament didn't keep track of numbers. He kept track *growth.* As he traveled from city to city, the Apostle Paul carried with him the memory of every church he planted. He was concerned for the health of each congregation. His heart for spiritual growth is the reason why we have his epistles preserved for us today in scripture--He continued to write to these new converts because he wanted people to turn to Christ *in order that* Christ would be formed in them.

Here is a sampling of Paul's concerns:

- When I could stand it no longer, I sent to find out about your faith. I was afraid that in some way the temper had tempted you and that our labors might have been in vain. (1 Thessalonians 3:4-6)

- My little children, for whom I am again in the anguish of childbirth until Christ is formed in you! (Galatians 4:19)

- Him we proclaim, warning everyone and teaching everyone with all wisdom, that we may present everyone mature in Christ. (Colossians 1:28)

- "... so that you may become blameless and pure, 'children of God without fault in a warped and crooked generation.' Then you will shine among them like stars in the sky as you hold firmly to the word of life. And then I will be able to boast on the day of Christ..." (Philippians 2:15-16)

Paul understood that scattering gospel seed is not enough. The seed must be nurtured, protected and tended or it will never undergo transformation. From its first contact with the soil to the final fruitfulness God longs for, it is the joint responsibility between the one who receives it and the one who plants it as well.

## The New Birth

As we examined in chapter six, Jesus used the metaphor of new birth (John 3:1-21). Nicodemus, ever the literalist, was flummoxed by the idea that a man needed to be born again. Jesus held his ground and stuck with the image. The Lord explained: *it takes a new birth to see the Kingdom; it takes a new birth to enter the Kingdom.* If Jesus proclaimed the possibility of new birth, we should embrace the idea that new birth is also the beginning of our growth in the Kingdom. Some people consider new birth the end of the process. Jesus's own metaphor tells us it's only the beginning. No one in the natural world remembers the circumstances of their birth--or even their first years of life. Part of the wonder of new life is the amazing (and rapid!) development of infants.

Each metaphor we find in the scripture is an invitation to meditate on the image and expand the application. Evangelicals have risen to the command *"You must be born again"* without fully embracing all the image implies. It describes reality: new birth must be followed by growth and development. Babies who do not grow and develop are either sick--or dying. We understand the idea of a new spiritual birth: why do we have difficulty with the idea of spiritual growth and development?

Consider child-bearing in the natural order of things. The arrival a child is preceded by the expectation of a new arrival. The parents understand that the family will be forever changed. They understand the need to prepare a nursery. Young fathers-to-be are gripped with the sober realization that the excitement of trying to conceive a child is replaced by the growing realization of a parental responsibility that will take decades to fulfill. Young mothers-to-be live with the growing evidence of new life inside them and the coming drama of labor and delivery. On the day of delivery ordinary life stops and everyone is focused on the birth. The family gathers, the child is born. Tears flow. Laughter blooms. Everyone is struck with the wonder of new life. Perhaps this is why Jesus used the image of celebration and feasting to mark the repentance and return of a lost sheep or son.

After the celebration everyone settles in for the joyful life-long task. New birth is not the end of the journey. It is the hope-filled beginning. The healthy baby encounters the new world. It is surrounded by light and sound, and by warmth and cold. The child has no way to interpret these sensations. The baby is driven by powerful urges for food, warmth, and security. Quite literally, this new birth underscores the need for learning a new way to live. The infant depends completely on the care of its family. If a child is not hungry the family recognizes that something is seriously wrong with the baby. Fathers and mothers notice every new trait: their little one begins to respond to touch and soft voices. Little eyes begin to focus; the baby turns the direction of its mother's voice. In those first amazing months of life a child's growth is exponential. We expect this growth. We look for this growth. Growth is the sign of health. Growth is the natural order of things.

So it should be with the new birth in the Spirit. All of these examples should find their analog in the life of a new believer. New life in Christ means entry into a new kingdom, the Kingdom of God! It is a near-fatal mistake to assume that we have nothing to learn, or even worse, that we can apply the old way of life to the new birth. It is a completely new realm, where the old ways do not apply--or could in fact be harmful. If a new believer has no hunger for things of the Spirit, something is seriously wrong with the baby. And not just the child--the family God has a role to play. In the natural world any parent who does not attend to on-going needs of the child is open to the charge of criminal neglect.

Yet in most church settings little thought is given to how to take responsibility for new Christians in their midst.

Many new Christians are told that because their heavenly destination is assured, then (somehow) the full work of Jesus has been accomplished in their lives. In fact, it has just begun. To be sure, pastors will pay lip service to the idea of spiritual growth, but in theological systems where forgiveness and heaven are the highest good there is no compelling reason to grow in Christ. It doesn't matter. Indeed, "growth" is frequently equated with "sharing the good news with others." The sobering truth is that many new believers exhibit all the signs of a healthy Kingdom-of-God baby but are met with neglect by their spiritual family. The result is individual believers whose hearts and minds were originally moved to respond to Jesus, but find no path toward spiritual formation.

### The Imperishable Seed

It was not just Nicodemus who struggled with the idea. The twelve followers of Jesus wrestled with another image Jesus presented: the seed of the kingdom. Because we have heard it so many times, we think of the Parable of the Sower as commonplace. Yet Mark's gospel suggests that Jesus considered the Parable of the Sower foundational for future progress in the Kingdom of God: "He said to them, 'Do you not understand this parable? How then will you understand all the parables?'" (Mark 4:13) This parable is the gateway to understanding the dynamic of spiritual formation, even though it is frequently interpreted as a description of the evangelism process. Many believers interpret the Lord's description of the soils as a kind of fatalism--which soil are you?

I encountered this parable immediately after I became a follower of Jesus. I just naturally assumed that I was the good soil. How could I be anything else? Sitting next to me on that occasion was a friend who had also just turned to Jesus. After we heard the message she wept and wept and wept. Finally she composed herself enough to sob, "I just don't want to let Jesus down. I'm afraid I might turn out to be one of those other types of soil." We both interpreted the Lord's story along static--fatalistic--lines. I assumed I was OK, while she reacted with fear and uncertainty regarding her fate. It never occurred to either of us that God had provided the seed, and *we* were responsible for the condition of the soil. To be sure, there are some faith traditions where this parable is received as an image of spiritual development, but there is no shortage of interpretations where we are asked to use it as a guideline to evangelism.

The Apostle Peter saw a path forward. He suggested a path marked by intentional obedience, sincere love, and an unshakable confidence in the seed itself.

> "Now that you have purified yourselves by obeying the truth so that you have sincere love for your brothers, love one another deeply, from the heart. For you have been born again, not of perishable seed, but of imperishable, through the living and enduring word of God." ~ 1 Peter 1:22-23

It is a two-part response: intentional obedience toward God and sincere love rest with us, while God's part of the mystery of the new birth is the power of the seed. New life in Jesus is something more than a resolution to follow him, more than human determination to become a better person. It really is a *new birth,* and Peter describes this new birth in terms of an "imperishable seed." It's true in the natural world: an apple seed can only produce an apple tree. Nothing else. Inside an apple seed are the instructions--the potential for an entire apple tree. Deep inside the seed is the DNA, and those instructions set the course for the seed. Yet, apart from outside interaction with the seed God's work remains only a seed.

DNA is not destiny. It is potential. Without the right soil or the right temperature, without enough water, the seed cannot reach its potential. The imperishable seed inside of each believer contains the possibilities of Christlikeness: to be born from above means that we have heaven's genetic code implanted within us. We are the soil: the choices we make shape our future in Christ. Becoming like Jesus is a partnership. Our choices are the soil, the DNA informs the outcome.

Peter was there when Jesus talked about seed falling into the ground. He heard the Lord teach about the different kind of soil and their effect on the seed. Peter saw first-hand the Messiah-seed planted in the hearts of the twelve who followed the Master. On the night Jesus was betrayed, Peter saw first-hand his friends scatter and run. In Peter's letter, written decades after Jesus ascended to heaven, Peter reflects on the potential of that imperishable seed. He encourages us to choose obedience and heart-felt love, because these ingredients are essential to reaching the full destiny of the seed. But it is our individual choice. Our response must continue beyond the moment we first meet Jesus. Each of us must ask, "how will I tend the seed inside of me?" Christlikeness is built into the imperishable seed. He graciously planted it there, beyond any merit or ability we possess. His DNA makes it possible for us to become like him, but our choices contribute to the outcome. That's the core of spiritual formation.

## Paul's Unfinished Labor: Our Example

This chapter opened with a representative list from Paul's letters showing that his concern went beyond mere numbers. Instead of counting "decisions for Christ" Paul's overwhelming concern was for the spiritual development of those who responded to his message. Of course, the great Evangelist wanted everyone who heard the message to respond--he welcomed the "big numbers," yet he wanted more: Paul wanted the new creation in Christ Jesus to find its fullest expression in people who looked like Jesus.

Paul's passion for spiritual formation is the very reason he wrote the letters we have in our possession today. These letters rarely deal with methods of evangelism. They deal with Paul's on-going concern for the health of the churches he planted. He understood that each believer has a destiny that leads to the image of Christ. He knew that healthy church families were vital to each individual destiny, and he knew that the master plan of evangelism required generation after generation of disciples who reflected the Master's image.

Consider this amazing passage from 2 Corinthians, where Paul defends his role as a Apostle by citing the burdens he had born on their behalf:

"Five times I received at the hands of the Jews the forty lashes less one. Three times I was beaten with rods. Once I was stoned. Three times I was shipwrecked; a night and a day I was adrift at sea; on frequent journeys, in danger from rivers, danger from robbers, danger from my own people, danger from Gentiles, danger in the city, danger in the wilderness, danger at sea, danger from false brothers; in toil and hardship, through many a sleepless night, in hunger and thirst, often without food, in cold and exposure. *And, apart from other things, there is the daily pressure on me of my anxiety for all the churches."* (2 Corinthians 11:24-28, emphasis added)

Among a long list of physical hardships and torture, he adds the burden of his stress on behalf of the churches he had planted. That stress impacted Paul physically. For Paul, the spiritual formation of those with whom he had shared the gospel was a goal so acute he felt their physical presence day-to-day.

Paul's letters are doctrinally rich with teachings about the person of Jesus Christ, the supremacy of the church, and the hope for resurrection from the dead. But these very letters demonstrate the primary fact that comes before theology or evangelism: Paul saw his Apostolic mission in terms of reproducing the person of Jesus in each person who received the good news.

- When Paul was forced to leave the newborn church in Thessalonica and flee for his life, he sent Timothy back months later to make sure the tender seedling was taking root.

- In Corinth, where a great number of people turned to Christ, Paul took on the added role as pastor and stayed for 18 months. Though our Bibles contain only two letters to Corinth, they point to a lively correspondence between Paul and the people he discipled. Some scholars suspect there were four or more letters between Paul and his church after he left.

- In Ephesus, the site of true revival and a city-wide conversion to Jesus, Paul remained for just over three years to care for those new-borns in Christ. Paul appointed his most trusted disciple, Timothy, to continue pastoral care for the church. As Paul began his long march toward Jerusalem and eventually Rome, he prayed and wept with the church leaders from Ephesus.

- His "Pastoral Epistles" are filled with advice for Timothy and Titus as they continued Paul's work, but these letters underscored the goal of spiritual formation. Titus 2:11-15 are among the most important spiritual formation passages ever breathed by the Holy Spirit, yet many (most?) followers of Jesus are unaware this passage exists. It presents a great calling for each of us in this life.

The great Apostle possessed a world-wide vision for the advance of the gospel. The gospel he presented contained the chain-breaking, life-giving news that each man and woman who turned to Jesus receive the DNA of their Lord. The new birth comes by the grace of God, but Paul saw that same grace as the life-line toward Christlikeness.

When hundreds turned from their Gentile ways and embraced the Lord of Glory, Paul understood that his labor was not finished, but only beginning. His unfinished labor is ours as well: Christ formed in us--*and* in the very people God brings into our lives. We are not only sons and daughters of God, we are also called to a spiritual parenthood that takes on the responsibility to raise others up in his image.

It has been often observed that we can be midwives in the process as the Spirit can brings new life to others. The same is true regarding spiritual formation: growth toward the image of Christ comes from God alone, but we dare not neglect the revealed truth we are the ones responsible to plant and water the imperishable seed in those we are called to disciple.

# CHAPTER EIGHT
# THE WORKS OF JESUS

I have a friend who came upon an automobile accident just moments after the collision. A baby was thrown from the car. He scooped the infant in his arms and began to pray for the child's life. He cried out to God for intervention until the EMT's arrived, but the baby was dead. Overwhelmed by the trauma of the event, he holed up in his apartment for days. You might think his depression came from the horror of injury and death, but his point of pain was his inability to do the works of Jesus in that situation. He was sick over his inability to represent the Lord in a crisis. He was not angry at the Lord: he was dissatisfied his own ineffectiveness.

There in his apartment, day after day, he prayed, *"You deserve better, Jesus… You deserve better."* He emerged from his apartment with a determination to carry the

Kingdom of God with him, because he was disciple of the Master. He had wrestled with the difference between a theology that acknowledged the possibility of God's in-breaking into everyday life and a theology filled with expectation that the Father *wanted* to break in. Since that watershed tragedy, his life has been marked by the consistent in-breaking of the Kingdom, marked by signs and wonders. His theology was unchanged, but his expectation had grown large.

When Jesus trained and released his disciples, he provided a remarkable level of equipping: "He gave them power and authority to drive out all demons and to cure diseases, and he sent them out to preach the kingdom of God and to heal the sick." (Luke 9:1-2) There's a similar description in Matthew's gospel: "As you go, proclaim this message: 'The kingdom of heaven has come near.' Heal the sick, raise the dead, cleanse those who have leprosy, drive out demons. Freely you have received; freely give." (Matthew 10:7-8)

It is important for every student of Jesus to wrestle with the gap between the modern life we live and the life demonstrated by Jesus and imitated by his earliest followers. Should we really expect to do the works of Jesus?

**What if heaven sent us a gift but we tried to give it back?**

Even among those who welcome the signs of the Kingdom (which include healing, cleansing, and freedom from demonic oppression) there is a tendency to consign the powerful manifestations of the Kingdom of God to another age. "The day will come," we are tempted to say, "when he will wipe away every tear from our eyes and set the captives free." This is quite true. The fullness of the Kingdom will be realized only at the end of the age. At the same time, we have the command of our Lord to represent the King and his Kingdom through powerful signs right now. Theologians call this the tension between the "already" of the in-breaking of the Kingdom and the "not yet" of its completion.

Our habit in recent years has been to settle for the "not yet" even though our present task requires heaven to break in now. Jesus instructed his followers to seek the Kingdom and order our priorities around heaven coming to earth. We live in the tension--the conflict--of this present age and the age to come. The challenge--the temptation--comes when we settle for the "not yet" as an explanation for our inability to carry out the mission. The sick, the hurting, and the hungry are queuing up because their need is now. Should we teach them to be content with the "not yet?"

New life in Christ should be a life of constant transformation. Because we follow an infinite Lord, our possibilities are infinite as well. Can you imagine a life of *being transformed into his image with ever-increasing glory?* You should: it's a Biblical description of your potential in Christ. (2 Corinthians 3:18) Becoming a follower of Jesus begins with at least three initial transformations: we must be born from above; we must acquire his character; and we must imitate his works. Most believers in North America have some grasp on the first, a faint hope of the second, and almost no concept of the third.

The gospel accounts are filled with the miscalculations, the infighting, and the petty pride exhibited by Jesus' original followers. Yet as Jesus prepared to leave, he charged these disciples with the impossible.

> "I tell you the truth, anyone who has faith in me will do what I have been doing. He will do even greater things than these, because I am going to the Father. And I will do whatever you ask in my name, so that the Son may bring glory to the Father. You may ask me for anything in my name, and I will do it." (John 14:12-14)

In the years after Jesus ascended to heaven, the Book of Acts records that the seed of heaven broke through the soil of their humanity in amazing ways. The first disciples demonstrated they were up to the task because the life of Jesus had been planted in them. Consider these three transformations:

1). *The first disciples were transformed by the new birth.* They really were a new creation. Heaven's DNA altered their very being. Timid, self-absorbed, working class men became world changers capable of threatening the Roman Empire just as their Master had done. We should ask ourselves, "If we have the family DNA, where is the family resemblance?" Perhaps the new birth is not accomplished by mere agreement with a few simple faith propositions. Many Christians are troubled by their past, troubled by their sin, and troubled by their futures. They've prayed "the sinner's prayer" and have been assured they are going to heaven, but they experience no change. If the power of God can assure our eternal destiny, shouldn't it be able to change our lives here and now? That was the record of the early church.

2). *The first disciples were transformed in character.* As a result of this new birth they demonstrated the character of Christ to a degree not possible by their good intentions or human effort. In our day, we are tempted to think we should "act better" because we are Christians. It's a trap: we will only "act better" as long as our will power holds up. That's usually not very long--just ask anyone who has ever started a diet! Eventually it will fail us, even as it failed the disciples the night Jesus was arrested. We need change from the inside out. Change flows from the new birth the way spring water flows from the source. Our job is not to try harder, but to drink from the source. The transformation of new birth finds its way into our character by our hunger and thirst for the stuff of heaven. A newborn infant without hunger or thirst is desperately ill: why should it be any different in our life with Christ?

3). *The first disciples were transformed by empowerment for ministry.* The Book of Acts reveals that the first followers of Jesus were startlingly like Jesus, in thought, word and *deed.* The history of the early church is filled with descriptions of ordinary people who declared the message of the Kingdom of God and demonstrated the coming of that Kingdom with powerful actions--just as Jesus had done. What they experienced in ministry at Jesus' side turned out to be merely a learner's permit. With the coming of the Holy Spirit the first believers discovered a transformation from the impossibilities of the flesh to the possibilities of heaven. What does it mean to do the works of Jesus? How we answer the question reveals our understanding of what it means to live "in Christ." In his day, Jesus had a high view of his followers. He believed in them more than they believed in themselves. It is still his day if we will let him have his way.

It is this third point that causes us to push back from the table, thinking, *this is over the top. It's too much to believe or hope for. It's beyond our reach.* Many Christians think it is the height of presumption to aspire to the works of Jesus. Yet we have the testimony of Jesus himself that he would like nothing more. Luke's gospel records the moment when Jesus received a ministry report from a large group of his followers:

*The seventy-two returned with joy and said, "Lord, even the demons submit to us in your name."*

*He replied, "I saw Satan fall like lightning from heaven. I have given you authority to trample on snakes and scorpions and to overcome all the power of the enemy; nothing will harm you. However, do not rejoice that the spirits submit to you, but rejoice that your names are written in heaven."*

*At that time Jesus, full of joy through the Holy Spirit, said, "I praise you, Father, Lord of heaven and earth, because you have hidden these things from the wise and learned, and revealed them to little children. Yes, Father, for this is what you were pleased to do. (Luke 10: 17-21)*

The phrase *"full of joy through the Holy Spirit"* is perhaps too tame. Eugene Peterson's *The Message* translation offers both "rejoiced" and "exuberant" to describe the Lord's reaction. He rejoiced because it was the beginning of the end for Stan's rule in the earth, because "ordinary" followers were the agents of this liberation, and because he delighted in the Father's method of doing this work in a way hidden from the eyes of the wise and learned.

The first disciples were up to the task. In the intervening centuries the people of God have sometimes lived up to the charge left by our Lord, and sometimes they have changed the task into something attainable by human effort. Every generation must wrestle with the challenge Jesus left us. The first disciples were up to the task. The obvious question is whether we are up to the task as well.

## 10:38 ~ The Believer's "Lucky Number"

Never mind that the website says "Sunday Worship, 10:00 AM," the worship team at my church starts up at 10:38, A.M. each Sunday morning. It's true that we've always been a chronically late group of believers, but *10:38* is intentional: it comes from Acts 10:38.

> "...how God anointed Jesus of Nazareth with the
> Holy Spirit and power, and how he went around

doing good and healing all who were under the power of the devil, because God was with him."

Call it our secret code. We want to underscore how Jesus did ministry and try to follow his example.

As you can tell from chapter three of this book, it's one of my favorite questions: *"How did Jesus do the stuff he did?"* If Jesus really is a worthy role model, shouldn't we imitate him? Jesus healed the sick, multiplied food, cleansed lepers, expelled evil spirits, and raised the dead. He spoke with confidence and authority about the Father's heart. He modeled a life of grace and peace, lived out in concert with the Father's will. But how did he do these things? Our answer sets the boundaries of *our* potential under the Master. Popular theologian Ricky Bobby suggests that "Baby Jesus Super-Power" was at work. Unfortunately, Ricky Bobby speaks for far too many of us.

I know what you're thinking: I threw a reference to the old movie, *Talladega Nights* just to be funny. I wish that were true. Just recently I read these words from a current Bible commentary (published in 2011):

> As a "superhero," Jesus has a vast array of superpowers--powers to heal disease, calm storms, defeat the demonic, love the unlovable. But one stands out in this passage: his sheer brilliance.

I wish I was making this up, but no, I read these words in a book from a reputable publisher. Perhaps the chatty, conversational commentator was just trying to be accessible, but he places the works and the character of Jesus beyond our reach. If Jesus did the things he did because he was the Boss' son, then his example is no example at all. We can stand amazed without any responsibility to imitate the Master.

In Acts 10:38 the Apostle Peter provided a powerful one-sentence summary of Jesus' ministry--including the hope that we, too, can be like him. I'd like to suggest at least four paradigm-shifting revelations from this one powerful verse.

**1). God the Father anointed Jesus of Nazareth.** Peter revealed that the source of Jesus' power was God's anointing. The concept of God's anointing is nearly lost in many quarters of the church. Yet, as we saw in chapter three, Jesus began his ministry with the simple explanation that "the Spirit of the Lord has anointed me" for the tasks before him (Luke 4:18). Peter simply used the same explanation his Master had used. If Jesus needed this anointing, how much more do we? Depending on your faith background the word *anointing* conjures up any number of images. Christians have interpreted this anointing in various ways, from a sacramental ceremony filled with symbolism to Pentecostal shouting and jumping. Behind either of these extremes lies a spiritual reality of Holy Spirit dynamism that breaks into out present reality. Whether it is a political stance that speaks truth to power (like Peter and John in Acts chapter 4), an inspired testimony (like that of Stephen, the first Christian martyr in Acts 7), or a powerful enablement (like Paul in Acts chapter 19), we need to recover a first-century understanding of anointing. Perhaps then we will recover first-century effectiveness in ministry.

**2). Even good works require the Father's empowerment.** Peter says simply, *"he went around doing good."* Who could be against "doing good?" No one--and that's part of the problem. Too often followers of Jesus are reduced to the role of religious social workers because we want do good, even if it's apart from the Spirit's guidance or assistance. It is a powerful temptation precisely because we can sally forth in our own understanding and strength, yet still do so in the name of God. Doing good apart from the Spirit's supernatural empowerment puts us at risk of self-righteous. We begin to think, "I did it--why can't you?" Living supernaturally doesn't have to mean constant miracles. It means the Holy Spirit is the wellspring of our thoughts and deeds. Jesus' do-gooding modeled something else: "Very truly I tell you, the Son can do nothing by himself; he can do only what he sees his Father doing, because whatever the Father does the Son also does." (John 5:19) Do we see the difference?

**3). Jesus saw ministry in the light of spiritual conflict:** Peter included the phrase, "all who were under the power of the devil." All ministry is spiritual warfare. Feeding the hungry is spiritual warfare; proclaiming the kingdom is spiritual warfare; healing the sick is spiritual warfare; and expelling demons is spiritual warfare. John, the beloved disciple said, "The reason the Son of God appeared was to destroy the devil's work" (1 John 3:8). Jesus saw the world as enemy-occupied territory. No human was ever his enemy. The work of liberation may involve standing up institutions and the people who run them, but even those who oppress others are themselves oppressed by the work of the Adversary. We need Paul's reminder that in ministry "we do not struggle against flesh and blood." Yet we *do* struggle. It pays to know where the fight is.

**4). The presence of God makes all the difference.** Like the anointing, the concept of doing ministry along with God's manifest presence is nearly lost in the church today. We will cover the idea of God's manifest presence in more detail in chapter ten, but for now we should recognize: we have settled too quickly for the theological idea of God's omnipresence. We mistake orthodoxy for *actual* presence. It is the difference between knowing the answer and experiencing the answer. The result is dry and lifeless ministry, yet we assert that because God is everywhere he *must* be in our works. We presume too much.

Peter followed Jesus day-by-day for three and a half years. He saw effective ministry modeled. He learned first-hand the possibilities of a Man yielded to the Father. He summarized his experience into a single sentence, a sentence so powerful it transformed his life. It could transform our ministry today.

Bible theory is one thing. What about life in the 21st century?

### Jessica and the Un-believing North American Pastor

Jessica lives among the poorest of the poor just north of Lima, Peru. As a very young child she fell ill, languished for a few days, and died.

In her neighborhood there were no telephones--no electricity, no running water. Her mother gathered the women in the neighborhood and began to pray. She sent others to find her husband, and still others to find the elders of the church, who showed up within a couple of hours and joined in prayer. After hours more of prayer, Jessica came back to life.

I met Jessica when she was about eight years old. Her mother told me how Jesus had raised her daughter from the dead. I suggested that perhaps her daughter had been very sick, but not dead. With typical North American smugness, I reasoned with the woman that God most certainly had healed the girl, but remained skeptical of outright resurrection. The woman became incensed and told me she knew very well that her daughter had died, and that Jesus brought her back. Jessica's mom was pretty angry with me.

Now, back in the United States, every semester I tell my students of the day I met a little girl raised from the dead. Then I watch them process the story--as I did when I first met Jessica. Then we talk about why North American Christians don't raise the dead. It's an important discussion because we are all tempted to think of Bible stories as just that--stories. Is it possible that the events of the gospels and Acts could happen through the ministry of ordinary believers today? In emerging nations all around the world, Christians are raising the dead in Jesus name. Why don't we see more of it in North America?

- **North American Christians don't raise the dead because we don't ask.** Death has the final word in our society: call the doctor, call the coroner, call the funeral home. Let them make the pronouncement and carry the dead away. Affluent societies are insulated from the dead. The dead are whisked away, cleaned, dressed and embalmed by professionals while we weep and mourn at home. It doesn't occur to us to stay by their side and ask God to intervene. When a woman named Tabitha died in Joppa, the believers asked Peter to come help. (Acts 9) They didn't accept death as the final word. Why do we?

- **North American Christians don't raise the dead because we don't see death as an enemy.** We attribute every death with God's sovereign plan, and comfort ourselves with superstitions like "everything happens for a reason." Yet the Apostle Paul makes it clear that death is indeed the enemy of humankind, "For he must reign until he has put all his enemies under his feet. The last enemy to be destroyed is death." (1 Corinthians 15:25-26) Death is real, and inevitable, but we have forgotten it is also our foe.

- **North American Christians don't raise the dead because because we have not learned**

**from Jesus.** Jesus taught by his actions as well as his words. Bill Johnson, pastor of Bethel Church in Redding, CA, reminds us that Jesus ruined every funeral he attended. True, his actions spoke of his own coming resurrection, but perhaps there was something else to learn from his example. Perhaps Jesus raised the dead because not everyone dies in God's perfect timing. A quick study of those raised from the dead in the gospels and Acts reveal that Jesus and his disciples intervened in the deaths of those who were young, or who died accidentally.

- **North American Christians don't raise the dead because we have pushed all resurrections into a single event at the end of time.** It is a day to be desired: the grave will give up its dead, we will meet him in the clouds. But our faith is about more than the end times. An illustration: when a local college-aged girl died of a mysterious illness a few years ago we sent a team to pray over her body. One local minister snorted, "why would anyone want to bring her back from the dead? She's happier with Jesus, isn't she?" The minister could think of no compelling reason for resurrection apart from the Last Day.

The scripture teaches us that we will all experience death. It would be foolish to think that Christians should stand against death every time it happens. Psalm 116 shares with us how tender and close the Lord is in the process of dying, "Precious in the sight of the Lord is the death of his saints."

Still, we need to be reminded that there was a time when there was no death, and there will come a time when death is no more. We live in the in-between time, and when Christians raise the dead it points to their Lord's mastery over all creation and his coming victory. What we see in the scriptures is the resurrection of the young or in case of unexpected accidents. At least to that degree, we should be ready--and willing--to ask.

We have read before the instructions Jesus gave his disciples: "As you go, preach this message: 'The kingdom of heaven is near.' Heal the sick, raise the dead, cleanse those who have leprosy, drive out demons. Freely you have received, freely give." (Matthew 10:7-8) The scripture presents the example of Jesus, Peter, and Paul, all involved in resurrection ministry. It's true that we will all taste death eventually, but it's not true that all death is for us to taste.

The Kingdom of God message should be met with Kingdom of God demonstration. Forgiveness, justice, mercy, community, healing, and yes, resurrections are all signs of the in-breaking of God's Kingdom.

Four bullet points aren't enough to change anyone's mind. But they should be enough to open the discussion: why don't North American Christians raise the dead? Believers in Asia, Africa, and South America do. We would be foolish--or worse, arrogant--to dismiss their experiences. In many respects believers on those continents are more familiar with death than we are. And more familiar with resurrection. This is no academic exercise. This discussion is important to our spiritual formation. We need to embrace all possibilities of life in Christ. Especially the ones that blow our minds.

# CHAPTER NINE
## THE GOSPEL OF THE KINGDOM OF GOD

They'll let anyone teach at some universities, and I'm proof of that. At the beginning of the semester in our peaceful little town fall freshmen descend on our small Christian college like autumn leaves: beautiful, but doomed. Poor kids: when I am assigned an applied religion course I receive 30 unsuspecting students who find themselves subject to the two central passions of my life with Jesus. It will take 16 weeks to share the two convictions that inform my life: the King and his kingdom.

In chapter one I shared the two bell-weather questions I ask at the beginning of each semester: "How many of you think Jesus is a worthy role model," and "How many of you think you can live up to his example?" These questions reflect Central Passion Number One in my life: *Jesus is the Master of Living.*

Just when they recover from Central Passion Number One, I subject them to Central Passion Number Two: the Kingdom of God is breaking into the here and now. I want them to reframe their view of Christ's work. What if the good news isn't about us going to heaven? What if it's about heaven coming to us?

With each new class I invite my students to engage in a spiritual exercise. Would you like to play along? Come into the classroom. Here is the question we must answer: *What if you woke up tomorrow morning to find that heaven had come earth? What would your world be like?* I ask each student to imagine heaven on earth. The rules are simple. Heaven has somehow come to earth. You're still you. Everyday life still goes on. If you're a student, you're still a student. If you have a job, you still go to work. But how, exactly has the world changed?

Here are a dozen answers from a recent class:

- "If Heaven came to Earth sickness would turn into strength."
- "God would be everywhere. God would give advice, spend the day with you, make sure

everyone was fed, and most importantly share his wisdom with us all."

- "Heaven's nature would begin to alter the workings of the earth and wipe out the impure creations of man."

- "No one would be lonely or without a companion."

- "Life with my daughter would change for the better. I would not feel that sense of silent discrimination from those who live in glass houses... we would not be the topic of whispers about a situation people truly know nothing of. We would not suffer judgments from those people with ample imperfections of their own."

- "This little town, what some would call a boring place, would flourish with excitement and love and unified happiness that we were living amongst the living God."

- "No one would have to suffer because in God's home you can find everything you need."

- "Famine would be completely erased. Sadness would be no more. Not one tear would be shed"

- "If heaven came to earth it would be a continuing cycle of great accomplishment."

- "The people on earth would be 100% stress free. No one would ever need to worry about anything at all... They would laugh and carry on as if they had no sense of time or worry... the normal stress I feel in my chest and head would be gone."
- "How could you be sad with so much love and compassion around you?"
- "Heaven is where you can go to be yourself and to be with Jesus."

Can you feel hope rising within you? Most people have the kingdom seed within their hearts. They intuitively know what the coming of God's kingdom looks like. In the ensuing weeks these students find their gospel turned upside down. The good news isn't solely about going to heaven when you die, it's about what Jesus has done to bring heaven here to earth.

Sometimes we spend the entire semester on Matthew 5, 6, & 7 (also known as *The Sermon on the Mount*). It's astonishing how many students think no one could ever put Jesus' words into practice. It's more astonishing still how many people think that because his words are poetic or beautiful that he somehow didn't expect us to give them a try. Recently one well-meaning student told me "Jesus preached this sermon in order to prove to us that we couldn't possibly do any of that stuff." Really? Would the greatest teacher who ever lived simply come to point out what losers we really are? Would God send his Son on a mission designed to fill us with shame and inadequacy?

That's the most challenging part of this spiritual exercise. These students intuitively long for the beauty, the grace, and hope of heaven. Why do they believe they must wait a lifetime to experience His good gifts?

How about you?

### Discovering the Kingdom of God:

I have a confession to make: I had been a Christian for years before I ever heard the gospel.

One night at summer camp on the shore of Lake Geneva, Wisconsin, I listened to the story of a God who loved the world so much he sent his only son to pay the price for other people's sin. My sin. I believed the message, I prayed the prayer and asked Jesus into my heart. It was five years later when I began to discover that the good news was so much better than I had been told. I've been discovering more and more of the gospel ever since.

Most Christians know that the word "gospel" means *good news*. But what exactly is the news? Over the years of my walk with Jesus I've discovered that the news is so much better than what people told me at first. Jesus had a precise message in mind when he began to proclaim the gospel. If you decide to investigate the *content* of the word "gospel" the first discovery you'll make is the connection with the phrase, "Kingdom of God." Let's look at the record of the New Testament.

- John the Baptist prepared the way for Jesus by preaching the Kingdom of God (Matthew 3: 1-2).
- The very first message Jesus shared was message of the Kingdom of God (Mark 1: 14-15).
- Jesus said the reason he came to Earth was to preach the Kingdom of God (Luke 4:43).
- He said the new birth was the way to enter the Kingdom of God (John 3:5).

That's all four gospels, and we're just getting started:

- The book of Acts opens *and* closes with the Kingdom of God (Acts 1:3 & 28:31).
- The Kingdom of God was Paul's message from Corinth to Ephesus to Rome (It's everywhere-- look for it!).
- The book of Hebrews describes a kingdom that can never be shaken (Hebrews 12:28).

- Peter and James declare that the Kingdom of God is the destiny of all believers (1 Peter 2:9-10 and James 2:5).

- The Holy Spirit inspired more than 150 references to God's Kingdom in the pages of the New Testament.

- In the Old Testament the rule and reign of God (that's the Kingdom) is displayed in the Exodus event, the golden age of Israel under Kings David and Solomon, and in the IMAX-vision of Isaiah's prophecies. The Bible is a Kingdom of God book.

If the words "Kingdom of God" seem awkward when they appear after the word "gospel" perhaps it's because we have shortened the gospel to mean exclusively redemption from sin and going to heaven. The rediscovery of the gospel of the Kingdom of God, along with Jesus' commission to "make disciples and teach them to obey" stand as the greatest needs in the North American church today. Discipleship under the Masters' hand and maturity in Christ depend on the gospel of the Kingdom of God.

**The gospel of the Kingdom of God differs radically from the gospel of Go-To-Heaven-When-You-Die**

We have confused Heaven with the Kingdom. Heaven is a great place. I'll get there someday because Jesus paid the price, but in the meantime Heaven is breaking into the here and now. I believe we have become preoccupied Heaven when we should be looking for how God is bringing his Kingdom to Earth. In the Sermon on the Mount Jesus taught us to pray, "Let your Kingdom come, let your will be done on earth as it is in Heaven." (Matthew 6:10) Jesus said plainly that God's Kingdom should be our highest priority: "Seek first the Kingdom of God." (Matthew 6:33) Do we really think he meant that we should place going to heaven after we die as our highest earthly priority?

[One note of explanation is needed here. Matthew's gospel usually prefers the phrase "Kingdom of Heaven." You can understand why many people have interpreted these words to mean Heaven itself, but if you compare the Kingdom of Heaven passages in Matthew with the Kingdom of God passages in Mark and Luke it becomes clear they are interchangeable. The reason for these two phrases is one of demographics. Most Bible scholars believe Matthew's gospel was written for a primarily Jewish audience. The Jews of the first century were very careful about using God's name, or even the noun, God. Instead, they substituted Heaven, because everyone in the Hebrew nation understood that heaven was where God set is throne. So Matthew's uses of Kingdom of Heaven are a courtesy to his primary audience-- the people of Israel.]

The Kingdom of God is the true context for discipleship. No serious student of Jesus ignores the teaching or demonstration of the Kingdom. Yes: demonstration. Jesus explained his actions in terms of the Kingdom of God. Healing, deliverance, and feeding the masses were all signs of the Kingdom of God. The world longed for the rule and reign of God to come to Earth. They received their answer in the actions and teaching of Jesus. In his absence Jesus expects us to demonstrate and explain God's Kingdom today. To be about the Kingdom is to be about the Father's business.

Perhaps one reason the church struggles in the area of spiritual formation is that we are not making disciples of the Kingdom. In our enthusiasm over God's forgiveness and mercy, we have overlooked his purposes and plans. Everyone who trusts in God can expect to go to heaven, but Jesus is after more than eternal reward. He wants us to join him in the family business. Receiving God's forgiveness and mercy--as wonderful as they are--can keep us focused on ourselves.

When we are focused on God's kingdom we find ourselves immersed in his priorities. Here's a modern illustration:

### Discovering God's Priorities: a True Parable:

*The taxi driver watched while we emptied our pockets, shoveling money and tears toward people we barely knew...*

I'll never forget my first trip to Peru. As a wealthy North American I had traveled the world previously. I had stayed at the finest hotels and soaked up the sun on privately-owned beaches manicured by Marriott and Hilton. This trip was different. I had gone to Peru share the good news of the Kingdom of God. I lived among the people of Lima and worked with them each day. We stayed in a modest hotel and ate our meals in neighborhood restaurants with new-found Peruvian friends. We encountered Peruvian believers who owned only a single pair of shoes and just one Bible. This is nothing new. Countless North Americans have had their world rocked when they discover the economic needs of others around the world. But I caught a glimpse of Kingdom of God on the very last night of the trip.

Our translators had been with us for ten days. We had spent more time with them than anyone else in Peru. As we waited for a midnight plane to take us home we invited our translators to one last meal together. We chatted like old friends and basked in the romance of a very short visit. Then it was time to head for the airport. Our translators, three young Peruvian sisters in Christ, hailed a couple of taxis and negotiated the price with the cabbies. As they turned to say their final good-byes, a revelation swept over the North American team: we were going home: *all of our Peruvian money would be worthless in a few hours.*

There was only one sensible solution. Give it away. The taxi drivers watched while we emptied our pockets, shoveling money and tears toward people we had only known a few days. We searched for every coin, each paper bill: whatever might be of benefit to our new friends. If someone was watching from the sidewalk it made no sense: there was an awkward and mad scramble to give it all away. There was no accounting. There were no instructions. No strings attached. As "employees" the translators had already been paid in full. Now the affections of our hearts and our imminent departure commanded a different kind of transaction. That night we began to understand radical generosity. We were living a Kingdom parable.

What if your money's no good where you're going? The old rules no longer apply, new priorities become urgent. The way you see the world has changed. Others may call you foolish, but you don't care, because your priorities have changed. They had become aligned with the Father's values.

This is only one picture of many from a life-changing revelation for me. Jesus is the King of an entirely different Kingdom, a realm with another language, another way of life, a different culture. God wasn't kidding when he said that his ways are not our ways.

## His Final Instructions

To understand the importance of the Kingdom message in Jesus' teaching, consider the Lord's actions and words at the very end of his earthly ministry, in the 40 days after his resurrection. Jesus chose to remind his friends about the message he had announced from the very beginning: the gospel of the Kingdom of God.

We would do well to remember that the resurrection was not a one-time event. Jesus remained on the earth forty days after his resurrection and appeared to his closest followers time and again. While many of us may be familiar with the details of Easter Sunday--the empty tomb, the fear and confusion, the bewildered joy of seeing Jesus alive again-- most of us are a bit fuzzy on the forty-day stretch after his resurrection.

He spent those final days teaching about the Kingdom of God (Acts 1:3). In the few days remaining with his friends, the Kingdom of God was still his passion. The subject most important to Jesus during that time was *the Kingdom of God.* This should not surprise us. Before Jesus began his ministry, John the Baptist declared that the Kingdom of God was close at hand. In his earthly ministry Jesus himself preached the gospel of the Kingdom of God. Now, with just a few days remaining with his friends, the Kingdom of God is still his passion. Have you ever had to give last-minute instructions? Imagine you were leaving (as Jesus was) until an undetermined day of your return: what would you say? What important words could you leave with your best friends? Jesus chose to remind his friends about the message he had announced from the very beginning: the gospel of the Kingdom of God.

The irrepressible E. Stanley Jones (Methodist missionary to India and friend of Mahatma Gandhi) was obsessed with the Kingdom of God:

> "I find myself with an inner compulsion, bolstered with confidence by the fact that the best and most influential man who ever lived, Jesus Christ, made the kingdom of God his central emphasis. I can't go very wrong if I stick close to him. If I fail I fail in the right

direction. I would rather fail with him than succeed
with anyone else."

Jones provided the most concise definition of the
Kingdom possible: "The Kingdom of God is Christlikeness
universalized." There's a connection between the good news
of God's Kingdom and our ability to embrace spiritual
transformation. God's kingdom is where every member is
part of a the royal family, each one growing more and more
into a regal family likeness.

> "But you are a chosen people, a royal priesthood, a
> holy nation, God's special possession, that you may
> declare the praises of him who called you out of
> darkness into his wonderful light. Once you were not
> a people, but now you are the people of God; once
> you had not received mercy, but now you have
> received mercy." (1 Peter 2:9-10)

Peter saw what Jesus proclaimed: individual believers
with a royal destiny--quite literally a nation of sons and
daughters of the King, with Jesus in first place as the
firstborn, older brother. His response was to encourage God's
people to recognize their identity and see the possibilities of
holy living in whatever their situation in life: slave or free,
male or female, child or adult.

## It's Time to Dump John 3:16

I hate bumper stickers, even when I agree with them. How can anything important be reduced to so few words? Our media soaked, marketing driven age has created a sound-bite generation. We have been trained to reduce life and death thoughts into catch phrases and slogans.

It's even true in the church, where for the last 60 years the most popular verse in the Bible has been John 3:16, "For God so loved the world that he gave his one and only Son, that whoever believes in him shall not perish but have eternal life." It's been the go-verse for outreach because it speaks of God's sacrificial love, our need for faith, and the promise of eternal life. I'm in favor of all those things--they are all true. Still, there is a danger in quoting John 3:16 apart from the gospel of the Kingdom of God. It reduces the good news to something Jesus never intended.

It's time to stop using John 3:16 apart from the gospel of the Kingdom of God. If Jesus commissioned us to announce the Kingdom and make disciples of the King, we should give people the full story. Anything less is dishonest. John 3:16 isn't even the full story of the conversation between Jesus and Nicodemus, why have we tried to shrink the Kingdom call into those 26 words?

Here are four drawbacks to shrinking the gospel into John 3:16:

- **Our embrace of John 3:16 means we have distorted the God's love, and his call for us to love in return.** Make no mistake: *God is love.* Who could be against love--especially the perfect love of the Father? But the love of God goes beyond his sacrifice and empowers us to respond. His love teaches us to love. His love is modeled in the life of Jesus--not just his death. Most important, when we use John 3:16 for outreach we fail to communicate the first and greatest commandment, that we should love the Lord our God with all our heart, soul, mind, and strength.

**Our embrace of John 3:16 means we have distorted the life-changing responsibility of belief.** Faith is vital to our entry into the Kingdom of God, but in our day *belief* has been reduced to *agreement.* True faith is a dangerous, life-changing force that causes us to die to ourselves and the old way of life. True faith causes us to count our lives as lost for the sake of gaining God's Kingdom. The kind of faith presented in a bumper-sticker application of John 3:16 asks simply for the nodding of our heads.

- **Our embrace of John 3:16 means we have traded the promise God's vast Kingdom for simply living a long time.** I'm so glad I will live forever. I've bet my eternal destiny on the life, death, and resurrection of Jesus. Yet when we reduce the gospel to everlasting life, we have presented a false reward. Imagine someone attained everlasting life apart from the love of God or transformation into Christlikeness--what would this do someone's soul? What if we got to live forever but didn't like the life we got to live? Jesus has a different definition of eternal life than simply beating death: "Now this is eternal life: that they know you, the only true God, and Jesus Christ, whom you have sent." (John 17:3) Eternal life is relationship with our Creator, knowing him and being known by him. To be present with God is to leave this life behind.

- **Finally, our embrace of John 3:16 means we have failed to make disciples. The Great Commission has become the Great Omission.** We have taken the methods of salesmanship and used them for an evangelism that misrepresents the gospel Jesus announced. It is a bait-and-

Ray Hollenbach

switch, without the call to switch. We should ask ourselves what kind of disciples have we made? For the last 60 years in North America the answer is that we have fallen short of the Lord's commission to us.

It's not a drive-by gospel. The Kingdom of God doesn't fit on a bumper sticker.

In the 1960's and 70's evangelism in North America exploded with tracts and methodologies that asked people to consider, "If you died tonight, how do you know for sure you'd go to heaven?" The focus was on the atoning, sacrificial death of Jesus. What Jesus did at the cross no one else could have done: he paid the debt of sin for all the world. Apart from his sacrifice, peace with God is not possible. However the unintended consequence of this approach to evangelism was a fixation on heaven to the exclusion of spiritual formation. To be fair, all these methodologies recommended Bible reading and church membership. Crusade-type evangelistic ministries worked hard to ensure that local churches would be on hand for follow-up with those who made decisions for Christ. The nature of their evangelistic appeal, however, made anything beyond "accepting Jesus as your personal Lord and Savior" an optional step. There was simply no compelling reason to become a follower of Jesus, the Master of Life.

More recently people like Todd Hunter, a bishop in the Anglican church of North America, have suggested a change in our approach to presenting the gospel. Instead of placing the focus entirely on the afterlife, Hunter recommends asking, "What If you knew you were going to live tomorrow?" Hunter invites us to move beyond "belief" in a set of faith propositions about Heaven and suggests "Christianity is a life, not merely a secure death."

What if we chose Matthew 11:28-30 for their outreach verse instead of John 3:16? How would these verses impact our view of discipleship, and our hope of spiritual transformation?

> Come to me, all you who are weary and burdened, and I will give you rest. Take my yoke upon you and learn from me, for I am gentle and humble in heart, and you will find rest for your souls. For my yoke is easy and my burden is light.

From their very introduction to Jesus, new converts would understand that the Master of living invites them into an on-going relationship that will equip them for the day-to-day, give them hope for life-change, *and* secure their eternal destiny. Many of us have had to rediscover the gospel.

Imagine a new generation of believers who hear the gospel of the Kingdom of God from the very beginning, unafraid to follow Jesus.

William Law, a master of spiritual formation in the 18th century put it directly: "If you have not chosen the kingdom of God first, it will in the end make no difference what you have chosen instead."

This is the message of the King and his Kingdom. Jesus, the King, demonstrates the possibilities of a life lived in concert with the Father. While no one will attain sinless perfection, the path to Christlikeness becomes a real possibility. When we fail, we have an Advocate with the Father, One who has paid sin's debt, so we have the confidence of our place in God's family. When the Adversary whispers in our ear that we are failures and disappointments to God, we have an Older Brother who is not ashamed to call us brothers and sisters, even in our weakness. When we condemn ourselves and are tempted to isolate ourselves from fellowship with God, we have the Shepherd of our souls who will leave the 99 and bring us back into the fold, because he is responsible for not only our death, but also our lives here and now.

# PART THREE:
# PUTTING THE ANSWERS TO WORK

# CHAPTER TEN
## I AM WITH YOU, ALWAYS

One day I left my cell phone in a friend's office. When my daughter sent a text message soon after, my friend thought it would be fun to respond to the text and pretend to be me. After an exchange of just two messages my daughter texted back, **"Who is this really?"**

She knew my voice. Even though she was apart from me and limited to the shorthand of text messaging, she was not fooled by an impostor.

One sure sign that we are becoming followers of Jesus is our ability to distinguish his voice from others. Jesus said simply, "My sheep know my voice." Yet Christians are filled with anxiety regarding God's direction and guidance. How can there be so many believers who struggle to hear his voice? When our gospel does not require relationship or presence it should be no surprise that believers have trouble hearing their Lord's voice. When our Christian experience is limited to learning the general principles of the Bible it should be no surprise that we have difficulty in knowing God's specific will for our lives about the everyday questions like *where should I go, and what should I do?*

What if the loving Father wants to speak into our current situation and give us direction for this very day? If we have never been told that he longs to have a on-going, daily relationship with us, how could we know his voice?

The comforting answer lies in daily, conversational relationship with the living God. This, too, is part of the gospel. The same one who said "My sheep hear my voice" also promised us a spiritual guide who will lead us into all truth. "All truth" is not just an accumulation of knowledge, it's everyday truth, revealing his will for us day by day. The Spirit of Christ is his active presence in our lives, eager to cultivate a relationship, a friendship, and partnership for living (John 14:16-29 is a good place to start). Because we have been warned that subjective experiences can lead us astray from the revealed truth of the Bible, many of us have been warned against listening for the still small voice of his presence. Despite these well-meaning cautions, every student of Jesus can learn to recognize the voice of God as we grow in a vital, everyday relationship with him as Father and friend. We need not worry too much about failure because his desire for daily communion is stronger than whatever errors we might make as we learn to hear his voice.

### The Distance Between Me and God

"God did this so that they would seek him and perhaps reach out for him and find him, though he is not far from any one of us. 'For in him we live and move and have our being.'" (Acts 17:27-28)

These words ring in my ears, "he is not far from any one of us." What is the distance between you and God? *Not far.* So many of us have been told there is chasm between Holy God and sinful man, and I'm sure that's true in some respect. Yet Paul spoke these words to people who did not care whether Paul's God was real or not. He spoke to pagans in Athens, with no regard for the holiness of the God of Israel or his son, Jesus. He told them that God was behind the events and identities of their lives and working in everyday situations in order to encourage them to turn his direction.

What is the distance between you and God? How far do we have to go to connect with him? *Not far.* It turns out that each day we live, we move, we take our steps, breath our breaths, we run our errands and do our jobs and live our lives--and all the while he is not far from any one of us. Do we know this? Do we feel it? If he is not far, how far must we go to connect with him?

How can we make space for him? The answers are as practical--and unique--as our daily routine. John Wesley was one of 19 children; his mother, Susannah, made space for God by pulling her apron over her head and taking a moment to pray. How can we make space for him? I have a friend who takes a ten-minute retreat from everything, including his own thoughts, just to sit in silence with God. I have another friend who uses a scripture reference as his computer's password; each time he logs on he recites the verse and asks for God's help in his work. Bill Johnson, pastor of Bethel church in Redding, CA suggests, "Since you can't imagine a place where he isn't, you might as well imagine him with you."

Whatever we may *think* the distance is, the testimony of the scripture is that he is not far from us. No one is excluded. How far do we need to turn? Some things we can only learn by doing. We will discover personally that the answer is *"not far."*

As I considered my need for presence of God I turned to John's gospel. At the very beginning I was arrested by a tiny word. It caused me to put down the book and worship with a fresh heart. My cup of wonder, amazement and gratitude was dripping from the rim again. I was reading along at the beginning of John's gospel when a simple two-letter word rocked my world. Perhaps it will mean nothing to you, but for me the lightning flashed and the thunder followed when I read the word, "**he**."

In the beginning was the Word, and the Word was with God, and the Word was God. He was with God in the beginning. Through him all things were made; without him nothing was made that has been made. In him was life, and that life was the light of all mankind. The light shines in the darkness, and the darkness has not overcome it. (John 1:1-5)

Did you see it? The Word, the Life, the Light is also a *Him*. He is alive and personal.

It's risky to share your personal response to scripture. *Huh? Others say. Yeah, so, what's the big deal?*

Like so many passages in the Bible, I am tempted to think I already know the truth: until the truth breaks into the room and becomes alive. What before had been only an idea came and sat by my side. The ink on the page is a mere cipher, a code devised by the cunning of men. When the true word was spoken the universe began to spin. There was no air to carry the sound. There were no ears to hear the command. There was simply the Word. And the Word was a

*Person.* Personal. Real. Relational. Alive. All I needed to do was make space for him--not my ideas about Jesus, not my knowledge of him.

For me, the big deal is the amazing metamorphosis from Word to Person. Too often what passes for faith lives only in my head--the paltry collection of thoughts from (honestly) a bear of very little brain. I suspect the Word became flesh and lived among us, in part, to reinforce that brains have very little to do with real life. He is the source of life.

Do you want to experience his presence? Stop reading. Put down the book, turn off the music, and invite him into the room. You won't have to wait long.

## His Presence, Tangible:

One great need among followers of Jesus is the experience of God's tangible presence. What good is it to have a theology that asserts God's presence is everywhere if we have no evidence of it? Has God gone on vacation? Is he like Elvis? Has he left the building?

From beginning to end, the Biblical narrative is filled with God's tangible presence. The first two chapters of Genesis are marked by his personal presence: God personally formed man from the dust of the ground, he kissed the breath of life into the first man, he walked in the garden with them.

At the end of the Bible, the book of Revelation depicts the intimate nature of God's personal interaction with creation. "Now the dwelling of God is with men, and he will live with them. They will be his people, and God himself will be with them and be their God." (Revelation 21:3)

From start to finish the scripture reveals the God who is present. He visits Abraham. He wrestles with Jacob. He talks with Moses face to face. He reveals his presence in the cloud and fire around the people of Israel. As Solomon dedicates the temple, God manifests in a cloud so thick that no one can remain standing or perform the duties of worship. Ezekiel saw God's traveling throne and Isaiah saw the temple filled with God's presence and glory.

In the New Testament the presence of God becomes something even greater: the Incarnation. "God arrived and pitched his tent among us." (John 1:14) This marks even greater intimacy and presence: God not only interacted with the world he created, he became part of that world. And he came to stay: the final words of Matthew's gospel are: "Surely I am with you always, to the very end of the age." (Matthew 28:20) Along with instructions to his followers, Jesus gives the promise of his presence. In fact, his instructions *require* the experience of his presence.

Today the activity of the Holy Spirit also constitutes God's living, tangible presence in the world. Jesus spent most of the final Passover evening instructing his followers to tune their eyes and ears to his presence mediated through the Spirit. When he tells his disciples, "I will not leave you as orphans; I will come to you. Before long, the world will not see me anymore, but you will see me," (John 14:18–19) he is indicating that the presence of the Holy Spirit is equivalent to his personal presence. Even when he was still physically available to be with his disciples in the 40 days after his resurrection, he began to give them instructions "through the Holy Spirit." (Acts 1:2) After Jesus ascended into heaven he appeared to the Apostle Paul personally, years later. Paul tells us his gospel came by direct revelation from Jesus himself. (Galatians 1:12)

Unfortunately, scripture also reveals that it's been the habit of God's people to be afraid of, or unaware of, the presence of God. As the people of Israel followed Moses in the wilderness, the smoke and lightning that accompanied God's presence caused them to plead with Moses to act as an intermediary (Exodus 20:18–21). The miraculous works of Jesus brought people face-to-face with the reality that something greater than Moses was in their midst. The reality that God was breaking into their well-ordered world brought alarm instead of acclaim. Religious observance always runs smoothly when divorced from God's presence. God's presence, on the other hand, usually upsets the tables, shrines, and instruments we have set in place. As C.S. Lewis remarked about his Christ-figure, Aslan, in the *Chronicles of Narnia,* "He's not a tame Lion!"

## A Confrontation of Grace

Paul, speaking to a group of people in Athens who were completely alienated from God, told them God was not far from any of them. Where did Paul get such an idea--that God is close to everyone, including outright sinners? I'd like to suggest that Paul got this idea from his personal experience.

If there was ever a candidate for the wrath of God, Paul's your man: a Pharisee who had missed the Messiah; a religious cop bent on dragging apostate Hebrews back to Jerusalem to face the music. Jesus took Paul's persecution of the people of the church personally: asking, "Why have you persecuted *me*?" Yet when Jesus confronted Paul on the road to Damascus it was a confrontation of grace, not judgment. The good shepherd had left the ninety-nine and gone after the one who had wandered away. You can read about it in Acts, chapter nine.

Imagine Paul, struck blind, sitting alone in a strange city, forced to re-think his religious convictions. He had given his life to study the Hebrew scriptures. He was considered a rising star in Judaism. He had been taught by the best and put his faith into action as an orthodox bounty-hunter. Then, after encountering Jesus personally, he sat in darkness and wrestled with one thought: *everything I know is wrong.* Years later, as Paul stood at the marketplace of ideas in Athens, he suggested that God is close at hand to each of us: the sensual, the cerebral, the religious, the skeptic, the clueless and the pagan. I suspect Paul could make such a statement because he had experienced the reality.

All it takes is one real encounter with Jesus to make us re-think our ideas about God. Not religious argument or philosophical persuasion, but *encounter.* I suspect that in the Damascus darkness Paul began to re-interpret the history of his people as revealed in the Old Testament:

- After Adam and Eve choose to eat from the tree of knowledge of good and evil they discovered their nakedness and tried to hide from God. Far from rejecting them, God himself went searching for them.

- When Cain was angry with his brother, it was Yahweh who tried to talk him down from the ledge. Even after the murder of Abel, Yahweh not only heard the voice of the victim, he placed a mark of protection on the oppressor.

- When Jacob cheated his brother and lied to his father, God did not reject him--though it would have been understandable. Instead, God revealed Himself at Bethel and said, "I am with you and will watch over you wherever you go... I will not leave you until I have done what I have promised you." (Genesis 28:15)

By the time Paul had re-calibrated his understanding of God, he was able to celebrate God's goodness and affections: "For I am convinced that neither death nor life, neither angels nor demons, neither the present nor the future, nor any powers, neither height nor depth, nor anything else in all creation, will be able to separate us from the love of God that is in Christ Jesus our Lord." (Romans 8:38-39) Paul, the legalist, had become the Apostle--not only of God's grace-- but of his presence and goodness as well.

Paul discovered that the Creator has always wanted to be among us. A loving Father allows nothing to get in the way. If sin separated us from the Father, then he himself provided a remedy. It's more than a legal transaction: the record shows that God will go to any length to be with us. If, as Isaiah says, "your iniquities have separated you from your God; your sins have hidden his face from you," (Isaiah 59:2) it is because we are the ones in hiding. He has not gone anywhere. He is still not far from any one of us.

How many of us need time and space to re-calibrate our view of the Father? How many of the events in our personal history would point to God's desire to be with us, if only the scales would fall from our eyes? I'm determined to find out. You're invited on the journey, too.

### His Presence, Tangible:

One of the shortcomings in the church today is the lack of God's tangible presence. What good is it to have a theology that asserts God's presence is everywhere if there is no evidence of it? These are important questions for us individually as disciples, corporately as the church. They go to the heart of whether we can put the wisdom and power of God on display for the world to see.

So the Bible teaches that God is omnipresent, but forget that: do you *experience* his presence? Amazingly, opening ourselves up to the presence of Jesus is not any different from developing a friendship with anyone else. He goes where is welcomed. He stays and develops friendships with those who order their lives around him. What, then, can we do to teach ourselves how to recognize and enjoy the presence of God? Let's consider at least five approaches to experiencing God's presence:

**The first step in experiencing the presence of God is to take the Biblical witness seriously.**

For example, consider this list:

- Then Moses said to him, "If your presence does not go with us, do not send us up from here. How will anyone know that you are pleased with me and with your people unless you go with us? What else will distinguish me and your people from all the other people on the face of the earth?" (Exodus 33:15-16)

- Where can I go from your Spirit? Where can I flee from your presence? If I go up to the heavens, you are there; if I make my bed in the depths, you are there. (Psalm 139:7 – 8)

- For where two or three come together in my name, there am I with them. (Matthew 18:20)

- But when he, the Spirit of truth, comes, he will guide you into all truth. He will not speak on his own; he will speak only what he hears, and he will tell you what is yet to come. (John 16:13)

These passages are well known, and that makes them dangerous: it becomes easy for us to dismiss them as inspirational thoughts rather than receive them as a description of reality. If we choose to acknowledge the reality of his presence, we must then evaluate whether our experience matches God's statement of the way things really are. Will we allow these passages to become normative for us? The plain message of scripture is that God is highly relational and wants us to experience an awareness of him daily. For those of us with a high view of scripture these verses should whet our appetite to interact with our Maker on a personal level daily. We have a choice: if our experience does not match the revealed word of God, we must choose to change our way of life and pursue the experience he has promised.

**Second, we should order our lives in ways that allow us to experience his presence.** The spiritual disciplines of silence and solitude stand in the forefront here. This was Elijah's experience:

> The LORD said, "Go out and stand on the mountain in the presence of the LORD, for the LORD is about to pass by." Then a great and powerful wind tore the mountains apart and shattered the rocks before the LORD, but the LORD was not in the wind. After the

wind there was an earthquake, but the LORD was not in the earthquake. After the earthquake came a fire, but the LORD was not in the fire. And after the fire came a gentle whisper. When Elijah heard it, he pulled his cloak over his face and went out and stood at the mouth of the cave. Then a voice said to him, "What are you doing here, Elijah?" (I Kings 19:11–13)

Or take the example of Jacob, while fleeing for his life, who learned a similar lesson only after God spoke to him in his sleep. In his flight from the wrath of his brother, Esau, Jacob stumbled into the grace of God, "Surely the LORD is in this place, and I was not aware of it." Jacob's experience is instructive: he was unaware that God's presence was all around him. One practical example: many of us are unable to start a car without turning on the radio. Why not seriously try silence or solitude for an hour—or a day? This is not mysticism, it is discipleship.

**Third, we should consider the joyful example of others.** Throughout history the witness is consistent: those who have been most aware of God's presence have experienced the joy and peace that flow from that relationship. Biblical examples include Paul and Silas who laid hold of God's presence even while in jail (Acts 16:25–

26) or John the Revelator in exile on Patmos. Brother Lawrence, a 17th century Carmelite, discovered that daily activities did not have to block an awareness of God's presence. He experienced "little reminders" from God that "set him on fire to the point that he felt a great impulse to shout praises, to sing, and to dance before the Lord with joy… the worst trial he could imagine was losing his sense of God's presence, which had been with him for so long a time." John Wesley, a buttoned-down English cleric, had experiences of God's presence that changed his life and ministry: his journal describes not only the feeling of his heart being "strangely warmed" but later describes that God sent him "transports of joy" again and again. Wesley's case is particularly instructive because in North America many church leaders emphasize scholarship over feeling, but Wesley had received the finest religious education his country could offer yet he did not personally experience God's presence.

When the Apostle Paul lists the fruit of the Spirit in Galatians, it is worth noting that at least one third of the attributes involve emotion. "Seriousness," however, is not a fruit of the Spirit. Two-thirds of Paul's description of the Kingdom of God in Romans 14:17 are "peace and joy." Although this chapter cannot provide a comprehensive list of great saints who experienced God's presence, it is safe to say that exemplary Christians manifest joyful feelings in response to his presence. Those who would dismiss joyful behavior as mere emotionalism somehow fail to brand dreariness and unhappiness as equally emotional expressions. They are the emotions of the *lack* of God's presence. The testimony of scripture is "you will fill me with joy in your presence, with eternal pleasures at your right hand." (Psalm 16:11) Perhaps this is why Richard Foster lists "celebration" as a spiritual discipline.

**The fourth approach to God's presence is the power of God.** John Wimber, founder or the Vineyard Association of Churches, said that power of God is in the presence of God. For those Christians who embrace the possibilities of miraculous signs and wonders in ministry, the secret is not to seek some special spiritual power, but rather the tangible presence of God.

The earliest followers of Jesus understood that their beliefs had no authority in the world unless they demonstrated the presence of God after they proclaimed the coming of God's Kingdom. In addition to forgiveness and reconciliation, healing and liberation from demonic oppression regularly authenticated the preaching of the gospel of the Kingdom of God. People who heard the message of the gospel of the Kingdom of God could also *see* the presence of God in their midst. When Peter and John were beaten, imprisoned, and released after they healed a lame man and preached the gospel, they joined in prayer with the other believers. Their prayer from Acts 4 (which we considered in chapter 6) is instructive because it illustrates the expectations of the early church:

Lord, consider their threats and enable your servants to speak your word with great boldness. Stretch out your hand to heal and perform miraculous signs and wonders through the name of your holy servant Jesus. After they prayed, the place where they were meeting was shaken. And they were all filled with the Holy Spirit and spoke the word of God boldly. (Acts 4:29-31)

This prayer, and the supernatural response that followed, indicated that the first disciples carried with them the expectation that the presence of God would be displayed *within* them ("enable your servants to speak your word with great boldness") and *through* them (stretch out your hand to heal and perform miraculous signs and wonders"). God himself answered the prayer immediately and in the years to come.

Decades later the pattern of God's presence expressed through powerful miracles was still the order of the day. The book of Acts records that the followers of Jesus continued the work of Jesus in both proclaiming the Kingdom of God and demonstrating the power of the Kingdom of God. This pattern continues today in most countries around the globe, with Europe and North America as the notable exceptions. One reason we consider Jesus an Impossible Mentor is we have settled for knowledge over experience. The roots of the problem go to our lack of expectation regarding the presence of God in our everyday lives.

**The fifth and final approach** to God's presence is so important it requires its own headline:

### God is Present in His Church

We should consider more than our *individual* response to the presence of God. The presence of God has implications for our life together as the church. Together we are the bride of Christ, and he longs to bestow his presence on the assembled church as well. It is popular in our day to embrace Jesus and shun the church. Popular, but wrong. For example, what if I told you "I like you, and I want to be friends with you and hang out together, but please keep your spouse far away from me!" Would you accept friendship on these terms? Such a friendship would be in peril from the beginning, and we put our relationship with Jesus in peril when we reject his bride.

The church is an expression of the presence of God in the earth. If we value the presence of God in our lives we should look for his presence in the church. Although it may stretch our trust in the written word of God, the Apostle Paul reveals that the church is "his body, the fullness of him who fills everything in very way." (Ephesians 1:23) In an effort to further strain our trust, Paul later says, "through the church the manifold wisdom of God should be made known to the rulers and authorities in heavenly realms." (3:10) Just as we are about to recover from the shock of these first two revelations about the church Paul asks us to consider the example of husband and wife as a mysterious image of Jesus and his spotless, radiant church. (5:25-33) Great theologians through the centuries have weighed in on the deep meanings of these passages, but it should be enough for each one of us to realize that Jesus has a high view of the church and manifests his presence through her.

Simply put, if we want to experience the presence of God in every way possible, we must encounter his presence within the church. This is a tall order because in our highly individualistic society because church-bashing is fun and easy. We have considered church attendance and membership to be matters of consumer tastes, as accessories to our lives. We assess everything about a church service—the music, the preaching, the seating, the people—everything except whether we met Jesus there.

The church is God's laboratory for living. He asks us to recognize and respect his presence in one another. "Anyone who does not love his brother, whom he has seen," says John in his first letter, "cannot love God, whom he has not seen." (I John 4:20) If we believe that the Holy Spirit dwells in each Christian, then we have an opportunity to experience the presence of God in each believer. In fact, the Biblical context for "grieving the Holy Spirit" is when we fail to show respect for others in the church (see Ephesians 4:29–32). That is, the Holy Spirit takes it personally when we fail to honor his presence in one another.

The lives of many believers gathered together in the church can authenticate the testimony of each individual life. It would be an easy thing for someone to dismiss the presence of God in an individual Christian as exceptional. But if the world is confronted with a society of exceptional people the only possible explanation is a common source of power and presence, namely God himself manifesting his life in a community of believers.

The scriptural witness presents us with a choice: are these pretty words, or a description of reality? "Where two or three come together in my name, there am I with them." (Matthew 18:20) The presence of the Holy Spirit was poured out on an assembly of 120 people in Acts chapter 2, and the earliest church in Jerusalem had the respect—and even the fear—of those outside the community of faith. (Acts 5:12–16) In short, anyone who desires the fullest expression of God's presence on earth should not give up on the church! True, most examples of church-life available for inspection today fall short of the scriptural vision, but God waits for a community of people bold enough to express his presence corporately as well as individually.

These five considerations are not an exhaustive list. They are merely the starting point. Can we have the same experiences of God's presence that are recorded in the Scripture? Are we willing to order our lives around the expectation of his presence? Will we discover the joy of his presence? Are we willing to recognize that his tangible presence could provide power for supernatural ministry? And finally can the church really become an expression God's presence on earth? These questions can only be answered if we are willing to move from lecture to lab.

## Substitutes for His Presence

Sadly, there are substitutes for his presence as well. If there is any hope for transformation as a follower of Jesus, we must be able to recognize and experience his presence. We must not settle for anything less than the experience of his presence. We must, in the language of advertising, accept no substitutes. Let me suggest two of these substitutes among Christians. We find them hiding in our everyday lives.

**The first is religious activity.** Activity is something we control. We can choose when to begin, how much to do, and when to stop. We can look back upon our own efforts and pronounce that God is pleased with what we have done. It would not be an exaggeration to say that most church work is characterized by human activity as opposed to the presence of God. How many of us return home from a church gathering and say, "I encountered the presence of the Living God?" Indeed, how many of us even attend such activities with the *expectation* that we will encounter him? Our use of business models for marketing and meetings are especially dangerous. We feel affirmed because we have drawn big crowds for God, even if he declined to attend.

Jesus ministered to crowds of people as well, but he also attended feasts with his friends, who sometimes happened to be tax collectors and sinners. They were people who valued his presence and truly longed to hear his voice. Who would confuse work and activity with friendship? Friends may in fact work together, but the difference between colleagues and friends is that friends share mutual affection and desire to spend time together apart from any "useful" task. When our religious activity is over, do we leave Jesus at church?

**The second great competitor to God's presence is our theology.** We often confuse knowing the truth intellectually with encountering the truth experientially. In our society understanding is overrated and personal experience is underrated. Our attempts to honor the Lord with our minds have sometimes caused us to become suspicious of any experience with him in our hearts. Make no mistake: Biblical revelation is important. It should be used to interpret and mediate our personal experience, but in the last two centuries Christian scholars have focused on rational exposition of the scriptures almost to the exclusion of personal experience with God. In the academy, and many pulpits as well, personal experience has been downgraded to anecdotal evidence and treated with suspicion if not outright hostility. This has resulted in Christian congregations who have no real expectation that God himself desires an intimate relationship with them. We must not mistake intellectual argument for relationship with God. The man who has experienced the goodness of God is never at the mercy of someone who has an intellectual argument against it. The Apostle Paul warned, "knowledge puffs up, but love builds up." (1 Corinthians 8:1)

Finally, consider these famous verses: "All authority in heaven and on earth has been given to me. Therefore go and make disciples of all nations, baptizing them in the name of the Father and of the Son and of the Holy Spirit, and teaching them to obey everything I have commanded you. And surely I am with you, to the very end of the age." (Matthew 28:18-20)

Jesus never intended for us to be disciples or to make disciples apart from the personal experience of his presence. The Great Commission, our call to make disciples, contains the promise of his presence. To make disciples apart from the active presence of Jesus is to make disciples who look like us, not Jesus.

# Chapter Eleven
## The True Operation of Grace

A parable: two students each received scholarships to Harvard University. Full rides, every possible expense paid. Both were bright kids, and both felt intimidated by the reputation of such a great college. They each thought, "I don't deserve to be here." One student studied day and night. She gave it all she had. The other student began to enjoy the thrill of college life: parties, the big-city nearby, and the freedom of being on his own for the first time in his life. By mid term the first student was still working hard, earning C's and B's in her classes. The other was failing every class and placed on academic probation. By Christmas the first student had earned a 3.0 GPA, but the second had flunked out of Harvard. Which of these two students laid hold of the opportunity given to them?

Of course the answer is the first student, humble and hard working. The second student was the object of gossip: "How could he throw away an opportunity like that?" people asked.

Imagine for a moment that the grace of God is like a full ride to Harvard: beyond expectation, every expense paid, a life-changing opportunity. Anyone watching these two students would conclude that the student who flunked out had thrown away a once in a lifetime opportunity. The scholarship to Harvard was a gift of grace, but the truth was that the work was just beginning. God's grace is something like this parable. He does for us what we could not possibly do for ourselves. What is beyond our reach is joyfully paid in full by Jesus Christ, but the work is just beginning. Why would we squander the possibilities of new birth in Christ?

Some people might object to the close association between the word, "grace" and the word, "work." God's grace comes with no strings attached, doesn't it? No amount of effort on our part could win his pardon. True enough—it's just not the whole story.

The whole story goes beyond the fact that God picked up the tab we couldn't pay: he invites us into his labor as the Kingdom of God breaks into the Earth. The Apostle Paul knew immediately that Jesus had laid hold of him for a purpose. Paul, filled with gratitude for God's grace and forgiveness, began to call himself "God's fellow-worker" (1 Corinthians 3:9) He considered the church in Corinth God's field, God's building, and he considered himself privileged to join the workforce. Paul was well aware that he had no moral standing to plant, preach, or pastor God's new church in Corinth; he was also aware that his "qualifications" were not the issue: "by the grace of God I am what I am, and his grace to me was not without effect. No, I worked harder than all of them - yet not I, but the grace of God that was with me." (1 Corinthians 15:10) What a strange combination of words: "grace" and "worked harder" all in one sentence.

Like the student who received a full ride to Harvard, we need to receive the grace of God for what it is: a calling to a new life.

Paul isn't the only Biblical example. Imagine the grace of God coming to one man, with a warning of worldwide judgment. Imagine that this one man--out of all the world-- had found favor in God's sight. You are imagining Noah. In an era when sin and violence threatened to spoil all of creation, the grace of God came to one man with the warning of a flood and instructions to build an ark. The grace was in the warning; building the ark was the response. God did for Noah what he could not do for himself. Noah responded by partnering with God to bring safety to every living creature. Tradition holds that construction of the ark took 120 years. Imagine 120 years of faithfulness in response to the grace of God. Noah's response to God's grace was sweat and effort that lasted longer than men or women live in our day. Here's the lesson: the only reasonable response to the grace of God is gratitude that moves us to action.

Some are given a free ride to an Ivy League school. Others hear a word of warning generations before the great and terrible day of the Lord. We all are given God's grace to become his fellow-workers.

### The Private Side of Grace

The Father communicates his grace in ways both big and small. When you're on the interstate, doing 85 miles per hour, you need a big sign: white reflective letters two feet high against a green background, shouting "Exit Here."

Late at night, when your baby is sick, you're looking for a much smaller sign, on a medicine bottle in print so small you reach for your glasses and turn on the light: "*Ages 2-4, one teaspoon every four hours, do not exceed four doses in 24 hours.*" You read the label twice to make sure you've got it right. Both sets of words communicate God's grace.

It's easy to see the public side of grace: it's represented in the cross. The cross is splashed across church buildings like so many interstate signs, signaling that the love of God is available to any who will stop. The news is so good it deserves a elevated platform. But those who see grace written large on the landscape might think that's all there is. Still, grace has a private side as well.

Consider some of the private sides of God's grace:

- Richard Foster points out the kind of grace you cannot see from the highway: "Grace saves us from life without God--even more it empowers us for life *with* God." The grace we receive at the new birth is only the introduction. Students of Jesus need grace for growth as well. Grace opens up the startling possibility that we do not have to yo-yo between sin and forgiveness. It becomes possible to yield every choice, every thought to God, because his grace can teach us to say "no" to ungodliness (Titus 2:11-12).

- Three times the scripture reminds us, "God resists the proud, but gives grace to the humble." Humility is part of the private side of grace. When the Father sees his children willing to take the low place in the family he pours out a special portion of grace to strengthen us in service to one another. Humility draws the blessing and favor of God. The same one who stripped to the waist and washed our feet rejoices when we learn to prefer one another.

- Dallas Willard's famous phrase, "grace is not opposed to effort, it is opposed to earning" reminds us of the proper response to God's saving work. The Apostle Paul understood the private side of grace as well: the famous apostle is the same one who described his task as one of "great endurance; in troubles, hardships and distresses; in beatings, imprisonments and riots; in hard work, sleepless nights and hunger," (2 Corinthians 6:4-10) all in order to share what he himself had been given. Paul had no trouble seeing the connection between grace and effort.

- What is the private side of grace? The private side of grace is the discovery that the new birth should be followed by growth into the image of Jesus. The private side of grace is when we begin to take on the family likeness. It begins when his children are old enough to understand that the Father sees what is done in secret--not in order to catch us in transgression--but to reward those hearts who joyfully follow his example.

Thirteen times: *"Grace and peace to you."* Each one of Paul's letters open with these words. Whether Paul was writing to the people of a church, to his "true son in the faith," or even writing to discuss the difference between slavery and brotherhood, his blessing is *grace and peace.*

Why would this man of God greet everyone in this manner? What is so important about grace and peace that Paul feels the need to speak the words immediately? Perhaps we could start here: Paul greeted everyone with "grace and peace" because he understood our on-going need for both of them. He was writing to believers, yet he wished for them more grace and more peace.

Part of the good news is there is more grace: grace for today, and grace for tomorrow. Grace for more than forgiveness--God wants to provide grace in the everyday: grace for growth, and grace to sustain. Grace and peace represent more than our need. They are the need of everyone we meet. Do we wish grace and peace on others? Do we have it to give?

## Jesus the Know-it-All

Consider the burden of the know-it-all: he must sit and listen to the mistakes of others: their opinions un-informed, filled with swiss cheese logic and day-old data. Above all, what he cannot understand is that, after he's explained everything so clearly, no one wants to listen. Apparently not everyone cares about being right.

When the know-it-all meditates on the life of Jesus, he is filled with wonder at how Jesus could put up with so many idiots. Unless, of course, Jesus had a secret weapon:

> "The Word became flesh and made his dwelling among us. We have seen his glory, the glory of the one and only Son, who came from the Father, full of grace and truth." (John 1:14)

If ever there was someone with a rightful claim to the title, *Know-it-All*, it was Jesus. Yet clearly, Jesus declined the honor. Turns out being right is not enough. Truth, meet grace.

Grace is love made practical. Grace empowers. Grace cares not for the argument, but for the people arguing. Grace has an agenda beyond the truth. Grace knows that the frustrated heart would rather sit on the sidelines and be thought wrong than be forced to run with the schoolyard bullies who are right. Grace turns its nose up at winning the fight and aims instead to win the person. Grace plays the long game.

Grace understands that merely knowing the truth is a slippery slope. The problem with knowing it all is the tendency to judgment. Even a smartie like the Apostle Paul recognized, "knowledge puffs up." It's so easy to wander across the border between truth and disdain, to pity the fools who cannot see what is so clearly true. Before we know it we have crossed into enemy territory, even though we were right all along. Sometimes the most insightful people appear uncaring and cold, like an oncologist who diagnoses the cancer but misses the human being standing before him. Insight is never enough. The line between insight and judgment is drawn by grace.

Jesus was always the smartest guy in the room, but he was also the most gracious. He embodied what he read in the Psalms:

> I will listen to what God the Lord says;
>   he promises peace to his people, his faithful
> servants—
>   but let them not turn to folly.
> Surely his salvation is near those who fear him,
>   that his glory may dwell in our land.
> Love and faithfulness meet together;

righteousness and peace kiss each other. (Psalm 85:8-10)

## The How-to of Humility

In my earliest years I attended a parochial school. I remember second grade distinctly because the "character theme" one month was humility. At the end of that month, in an assembly before the entire school, I was named the winner of the "Humility Award," but they took it away from me because I actually accepted the award!

OK, so the story is not true: but it illustrates the conflicting ideas Christians entertain regarding what it means to be humble. Where do we get our ideas about humility? If God gives grace to the humble, how can I eagerly pursue his best for me without falling into mere self-interest? Both Peter and James both quoted the Old Testament, "God resists the proud, but gives grace to the humble." They latched on to this teaching from Proverbs 3:34. It must be important. First, it tells us that God gives grace. Fair enough: isn't that what God is supposed to do? But this verse also tells us that God gives grace to certain kinds of people—humble people. Finally, it also tells us that God can withhold grace from another kind of people—the proud. Keep in mind that Peter and James were writing to believers.

We should be the kind of people who humble ourselves. On the other hand, if we do not humble ourselves, we may just find out that God is opposing us. I'm not sure what that looks like, but I'm pretty sure that it's not a good thing. Many believers are surprised to learn that there is something we can all do to bring the grace of God into our lives: we can humble ourselves.

Matthew 11:25-30 points to an important revelation: Jesus invites anyone who would follow him to come under his instruction and learn his way of life. Surprisingly, his first reason for calling us to follow him is that he is "gentle and humble in heart." Even as he offers the benefit of rest, he highlights his own personality--a gentle and humble man. The Teacher does not want to impart merely information, his first lessons are his very own attributes--gentleness and humility. It is a bold offer to follow him, and perhaps the boldest aspect of this offer is the unimaginable possibility that we can learn to become like him.

Jesus said, "Take my yoke upon you and learn from me." This image was common enough in his day: A yoke is a large collar which places the strength of an ox or horse at the disposal of someone else. We place our strength at his disposal. He will not conquer us, we must bow before him as a matter of choice. The path to becoming like Jesus starts with his invitation, "Come to me." After he speaks we can choose to accept that invitation by only one method: to humble ourselves.

In fact, on four separate occasions Jesus employs this phrase: "the one who humbles himself will be exalted." These passages are not simply repetition caused by the gospels re-telling the same story--each passage is unique (Matt. 18:4, Matt. 23:12, Luke 14:11, and Luke 18:14). Four times Jesus lays out the challenge: humble yourself. *But how?* I invite you to read each passage and meditate on each setting. Each passage teaches us the "how to" of humility:

*Matthew 18:1-4: Lay aside dreams of greatness and embrace dreams of dependency.* This is the highway of the Kingdom of Heaven. Jesus said that among men there was none greater than John the Baptist, yet the person who was "least" in the Kingdom of Heaven was greater than John. Living in the Kingdom requires God's intervention every day. We cannot make the Kingdom happen, we can only proclaim that the Kingdom of Heaven is breaking in, and then depend on Him to invade the ordinary with his presence and power.

*Matthew 23:1-12: Lay aside the thrill of recognition and find the joy of serving.* If we are honest we will recognize ourselves in the people Jesus describes--those who strive for recognition by the way they dress, or where they park, or by the titles they hold. It is thrilling to be noticed, to be selected from among the crowd for recognition. Meanwhile the servants come and go in the midst of all the clamor, quietly attending to the Master's business. But in the Sermon on the Mount Jesus reveals that the Father is the one who "sees in secret."

*Luke 14:7-14: Lay aside the thirst for honor from others and seek to honor others instead.* In fact Jesus tells us to honor those who cannot repay us. True, there is a time of reckoning and a place to receive repayment, but it is not here and now; it is later. Can we delay gratification or does our thirst drive us to be satisfied now?

Luke 18:9-14: Lay aside self assessment and depend on God's mercy. Jesus draws a picture of two men at prayer. The first mans begins his prayer with "thank you," but quickly tallies up the score of the game he has been playing. He has been keeping score all along and reminds God that he is the winner. The other man starts with God's mercy instead of self assessment. Score-keeping (and judgment) belong to God. Let's be careful. If we have a measuring stick, we will eventually be asked to stand next to it!

Grace is about more than knowing, it's also about being. If God wants to give me the grace to be more like Jesus, and if it takes a little effort on my part, then count me in. It's how we take the yoke. It's how we position ourselves to learn from him.

## Provoking God's Mercy

Are there any limits to human wickedness? Imagine a guy who practices witchcraft and seances, fortune-telling and necromancy. Picture him engaged in human sacrifice by burning his own children on altars of fire. Give him nationwide authority and influence, so that he not only practices these things, but encourages and trains others to do the same. Now, if there is room left in your imagination, envision this man finding a way to win God's affection.

Buried deep in the Chronicles of Israel is the story of a despicable king guilty of such things. Yet he captured the Father's grace and mercy by humbling himself before God. His name is Manasseh; you can read about him in 2 Chronicles 33. In the space of one chapter King Manasseh was transformed from a man who provoked God to anger to one who caught God's attention because of his humble heart. There is a lesson here for every student of Jesus: it's not that Manasseh simply experienced God's mercy, he *provoked* it.

The Father loves humility. It turns his head. Jesus tried again and again to share this secret pathway to God's heart:

"the one who humbles himself will be exalted." Jesus demonstrated humility as he lived in the low places of Israel's society. He portrayed children as exemplars of humble trust in the Father's care. He derided self-sufficiency.

Humility is an expression of truth and integrity. People intuitively hunger for humility in their spiritual and political leaders. I have a spiritual formation blog, StudentsofJesus.com, where I posted an article on practical steps toward humbling yourself. Although the post is years old, people find their way to it week after week. All over the world people enter search phrases like, "how to be humble like Jesus," and "how do we humble ourselves before God?" Their hearts are hungry to find the peace offered by humility. There is beauty in the humble way.

Humility is the sail that captures the grace and mercy of God. His ear is tuned to hear the weakest words of a humbled heart. In King Manasseh's story we find hope for everyone who has wondered if they could possibly grab God's attention. Here are four sure lessons from Manasseh (2 Chronicles 33) for those whose hearts are inclined:

- *Even in the midst of gross iniquity, God is still speaking:* (v10) Even after a long list of rebellious acts against God, the text reveals that God was still reaching out to Manasseh. If you've been told that God hides from your sin, you've been misled. Our sin is one of the very reasons God continues to reach out to us. He loves us and refuses to give up on us. But it's not just that his love reaches down; a humble heart reaches up.

- *God knows how to humble us:* (v11) There's a massive difference between being humbled by the Almighty and humbling yourself before him. God may arrange circumstances that bring us low in the eyes of others, but only we can lower ourselves before God. He can extend severe mercy but we remain in control of our own thoughts and hearts.

- Our hearts can move God's heart: (v13) This is an astounding revelation! God is not impressed by human power, wealth, or wisdom, but he is impressed by the human heart. When a man or woman chooses contrition, the Father tells all heaven to be quiet. Our prayers never have more power than when we take our proper place before him.

- Our humble example can influence the generations to come: (v25) Manasseh had a grandson named Josiah, who (as a child) sparked a nationwide revival. I like to imagine that Josiah heard first-hand from his grandfather the horrors of rebellion and the grace of humility. Our life-lessons can become the seed that springs up thirty, sixty, and a hundred fold in the lives of those who follow.

These are more than theological considerations, they are postures of the heart. They are examples. Jesus embodied the life of humility before the Father. It worked out pretty well for him. He demonstrated that the humble path leads to glory, a glory unimagined by the wisdom of men.

Even more than Manasseh, Jesus modeled the way of humility. Consider Paul's magnificent description of the humble way:

> In your relationships with one another, have the same mindset as Christ Jesus:
> Who, being in very nature God,
> did not consider equality with God something to be used to his own advantage; rather, he made himself nothing
> by taking the very nature of a servant,
> being made in human likeness.
> And being found in appearance as a man,

he humbled himself

by becoming obedient to death—

even death on a cross!

Therefore God exalted him to the highest place

and gave him the name that is above every name,

that at the name of Jesus every knee should bow,

in heaven and on earth and under the earth,

and every tongue acknowledge that Jesus Christ is
Lord,

to the glory of God the Father. (Philippians 2:6-11)

What is whispered in the Old Testament is shouted in the New: humility is the doorway to God's Kingdom. Humility spared Manasseh's life. It was the way of life for Jesus. It is no less the way for us.

## Infinite God, Infinite Grace

One day I received a phone call in my office. The conversation was long and complicated--and frankly, not very interesting. It seemed like the guy would never get off the phone, and I had somewhere to go *right now*.

We've all been in situations like this: late for an appointment, packing up our things while talking on the phone so we can bolt the moment the conversation is over. "When will this guy finish?" I thought. "I should have left five minutes ago…" and then it hit me: I was in my office, but I was talking to him on my cell phone. I could have left the office and headed for my appointment while he rambled on!

My real problem was not the long-winded guy on the phone, it was that everything I learned about the telephone came from a time when telephones had cords and using the phone meant staying in one place. It was a lesson: there are times when we must examine the things we think already know. We must clear the slate and begin again.

Followers of Jesus must see the grace of God through new eyes.

> "In the terrain of life with God, grace is not a ticket to heaven, but the earth under our feet on the road with Christ… Grace saves us from life without God--even more it empowers us for life with God." ~ Richard Foster (with Kathryn Helmers) in *Life with God*

One of the weaknesses of spiritual formation is that after we come to understand the importance of our response to God's grace, it's easy to get idea that God has done everything he's going to do. The rest is up to me: I must meditate, pray, serve, study, contemplate, isolate, and even celebrate on my own. Jesus showed me how it's done, died on the cross, paid the price, and now it's up to me to respond. There's a measure of truth to such thinking, but the best lies always use a bit of the truth. The reality is our constant need for his grace: God's grace is the disciple's fuel for life.

God's grace starts well before we come alive to his call; it is the power to forgive and save at the new birth; and it is the pathway to walk with him forevermore. As mentors like Richard Foster and Dallas Willard have pointed out time and again, spiritual disciplines are practices that put us into position to receive more of his grace. The disciplines are not spiritual hurdles to be cleared by the "serious" student of Jesus. The startling truth is that those who desire to live godly in Christ Jesus need *more* of God's grace than others who have no interest in spiritual transformation.

John's gospel opens with words of grace: "From the fullness of his grace we have all received one blessing after another." (John 1:16) Apparently the good folks who translated the New International Version were challenged by the more literal rendering of this verse, "From his fulness we have all received, grace upon grace." (New Revised Standard Version). The NIV substitutes "one blessing after another" for "grace upon grace." But why argue over translation? I believe John was searching for a way to communicate that God's grace is multi-layered. If we walk with him 50 years we will discover again and again the God who beckons us (in C.S. Lewis' happy phrase) to come "further up and further in." But take note: if we are determined to think of grace as merely a ticket to heaven there is no further up and further in--either in this life or the next. Why come to the shores of God's grace only to dip our toes in the ocean?

James 4:6 reminds us: "But he gives us more grace. That is why Scripture says: 'God opposes the proud but gives grace to the humble.'" More grace. Greater grace. All the more grace. I believe James was speaking from experience, not theory. I think he discovered the multi-layered grace of God as he learned to humble himself again and again. When we humble ourselves we position ourselves for greater grace. One sure indicator of a religiously closed mind is the firm conviction that we have this Jesus-thing figured out. The religiously closed mind is only interested in exporting it's brand of spirituality. We need to discover that it's impossible to drink in God's grace if we do nothing but tell others how to live.

What kind of Father would tell his child, "I've done all I'm going to do, the rest is up to you?" Our transformation is his work, accomplished as we present ourselves to greater grace again and again. If we limit his grace to the work of forgiveness, then forgiveness is all we will know. If we open ourselves up to his infinite grace then our destiny is the infinite God.

Infinite God. Infinite Grace. Infinite Destiny. How little I know about God's grace. Decades later I'm still discovering his grace is the air I breathe.

## The Lessons of Grace

You've already doing it, but usually unaware. Right now: take a breath. Breathe deep. Seriously--right here, take a deep breath.

Do it again. This time feel the air circulate through your nose; feel your chest swell, and instead of expelling the air with force, allow it to find its way out. The air we breathe reaches the smallest parts of our body--nothing is ignored. The air we breathe cleans our blood and strengthen every cell. The air we breathe is the grace of God.

The great sky is more than a home for the clouds--the grace of Heaven reaches down to us all. From all around us to deep inside us, from our lungs to every part of our souls, his grace is reaching you and me. His grace surrounds us and flows through us. We cannot live for more than a moment without it.

The reality of grace is all around us: every breath a parable, every moment sustained by him. Sitting alone or on a crowded subway, we can draw the lessons of Grace.

*Ubiquitous grace.* We have all received his grace. Sinner or saint, unconscious or aware, asleep or awake, we have received. We receive now. We will receive. His grace is for everyone, foe or friend.

*Unlimited supply.* We cannot use it all, even if we try. We cannot use all the air in the room, much less the sky. Great clouds of grace sweep over the face the earth, bringing wave after wave of our greatest, most basic need. What we most need we can never expend. Nor does he chide or limit, ration or withhold. It is his joy to give.

*A parable of love.* The schoolchild learns that as we breathe our body benefits and thrives: from our lungs to our blood, from the blood to the cells, airy grace first delivers what we crave and carries away our most toxic waste. His grace brings us his life, and carries away our death.

*Grace for all, because all have need.* He is as close as our need: waiting, filling, cleansing, bearing away all that is ill and returning again and again afresh in a joyful cycle of life. All this when we breathe, whether we know it or not.

It's always there for us to experience, if we just breathe.

# CHAPTER TWELVE
## MAKING DISCIPLES MAKES ME

Following Jesus includes making disciples. The path of discipleship includes the joy of helping others to become disciples. Some have mistaken the Great Commission (Matthew 28:16-20) as a call to evangelism while others have mistaken the Great Commission as a call to *personal* discipleship without regard to the welfare of others.

Of course, we should share the good news of Jesus' substitutionary death--he paid the price for us to be reconciled to the Father. But the good news also includes the promise that anyone who turns to Jesus should be taught how to obey everything he commanded. How many of us have considered evangelism in the light of raising up obedient followers of Jesus?

It's no surprise that our example is the Lord Himself. His proclamation that the Kingdom of God was breaking into the here and now also included "Come, follow me." When we encounter these words it's easy to think, "Of course, everyone should follow Jesus," but Jesus of Nazareth was an unknown teacher from the hill country of Galilee. In effect he told others, "I can demonstrate the good life." His message was more than information, it included the invitation to imitate his way of life. The Apostle Paul understood the implications of the Great Commission when he boldly asserted to the Corinthians, "Follow my example, as I follow the example of Christ." (1 Corinthians 11:1) How many of us are comfortable in making the same claim: "Imitate my life, and in so doing you will learn how to become like Jesus."

Pointing to Jesus is not enough. Our personal growth as followers of Jesus is not complete until we lead the way for others. It's part of Jesus' plan for us. Demanding obedience to God is not enough. Real discipling is about paving the way for others to approach the Father. Jesus not only insisted upon obedience, he showed his disciples how it was done. May God give us the grace to do the same.

## Can We Grow Without Making Disciples?

Jesus is full of surprises: How can the ruler of the world become an example of obedience? How can the object of worship himself become an example of *how to* worship? How can the perfect Son of God call others to follow him, and then demonstrate the way to follow? It's part of his genius, his glory, his nature. What's more, he not only showed us how it's done, he empowered us to do the same. The gospel record demonstrates Jesus lived a life of obedience to the Father and called us into the same obedience. But Jesus did not leave us to struggle with obedience alone. The Master Teacher, was also the Master Equipper:

> "I have much more to say to you, more than you can now bear. But when he, the Spirit of truth, comes, he will guide you into all truth. He will not speak on his own; he will speak only what he hears, and he will tell you what is yet to come. He will bring glory to me by taking from what is mine and making it known to you. All that belongs to the Father is mine. That is why I said the Spirit will take from what is mine and make it known to you." (John 16:12-15)

We are called to make disciples as well, to teach others to obey everything he commanded. Many of us see discipleship only in terms of following Jesus, and almost never in terms of leading others. And there's a personal risk: if we try to lead others, we run the risk of demanding obedience to Jesus from other people without actually equipping them to obey him. Both these challenges are critical to our personal development as students of Jesus. Our personal spiritual growth depends on coming to terms with these challenges. The destiny of others depends on our response as well.

How many of us receive the call to discipleship as a personal call from God to become a leader? We may come to him because we need a Savior, but when we choose to become a follower of Jesus we must also realize we are also choosing the responsibility to lead others. This is part what it means to follow him: we act on his behalf in the lives of others. It's more than "sharing our faith." It's taking responsibility for other people's lives until they are mature followers of Jesus. He showed us--in very practical ways--exactly how it works.

Jesus gave his disciples the tools necessary to live a healthy life with God. He did more than demand. He did more than point the way. He empowered his followers. He pointed to issues of the heart, as in Matthew 5; he included his students as partners in ministry, giving them hands-on experience, as in Matthew 10; and, as the passage from John

16 indicates, he introduced them to the Holy Spirit, effectively opening the resources of heaven to each of his disciples. What about us? As disciple makers, do we interact with those God has given us in the same way? Do we teach about heart-matters? Do we release our students into ministry? Do we introduce them to the Holy Spirit?

First things first: we cannot equip others until we believe we are called to lead others. It will not do to claim, "I have no one to lead." Jesus is our model: he came in obedience to the Father and simultaneously became a leader of others. We must do the same, and God has provided venues for our leadership: in our homes, among our friends, at work or school, or in our community. We were called to change the world by allowing God to change us *and* by becoming God's agents of change where he leads us.

Who knew discipleship would require everything we have? I suspect the Master did.

### Two Vital Needs of Every Christian:

When I told one of my best friends that for my (third) career I wanted to be a writer, he gave me life-changing advice: "Try to imagine talking about your subject every single day for two years. If the idea still thrills you, you've found your topic." Becoming a disciple of Jesus--and making disciples of others--takes me deeper and deeper into life with God. These are the two great needs of every Christian: to be a disciple and to make disciples. When I encounter familiar old Bible passages on discipleship, they seem constantly-fresh, filled with life: always revealing the new possibilities of following the Lord.

Will you allow me to share a few of these ever-fresh passages? Here are **three foundational passages** for walking in our two vital needs:

Now the eleven disciples went to Galilee, to the mountain to which Jesus had directed them. And when they saw him they worshiped him, but some doubted. And Jesus came and said to them, "All authority in heaven and on earth has been given to me. Go therefore and make disciples of all nations, baptizing them in the name of the Father and of the Son and of the Holy Spirit, teaching them to observe all that I have commanded you. And behold, I am with you always, to the end of the age." (Matthew 28:16-20)

- If heaven is the ultimate goal of the gospel, then discipleship is merely an option, like a choice in the cafeteria. Discipleship is not a choice, it's the mission. There is something lacking in each one of us until we become disciples and until we make disciples of others.

- Discipleship is open to anyone willing to worship Jesus. Intellectual curiosity is not the ticket in, nor are good works. And here is the really good news: doubt does not disqualify you from worship.

- At the place of worship we discover that Jesus considers us partners in his mission. He never intended the original twelve disciples to be the only ones: he intended they would reproduce themselves. Amazingly, he intends the same for us as well.

For those whom he foreknew he also predestined to be conformed to the image of his Son, in order that he might be the firstborn among many brothers. (Romans 8:29)

- The good news is better than we think: the Father intends that each of us can become conformed to the image of his son. This is staggering: if we are disciples of Jesus, the Father has set a destination for each of us--Christlikeness!

- Jesus is unique: the only begotten of the Father. Yet that same Father is determined to have a large family. He sends a spirit of adoption into our hearts. We see him as our true Father and we discover our older brother is none other than the Lord of Glory.

- When we first heard the gospel--presented as Jesus' sacrificial death on our behalf--how many of us imagined the Father had a destination in mind better than Heaven itself?

At that time Jesus declared, "I thank you, Father, Lord of heaven and earth, that you have hidden these things from the wise and understanding and revealed them to little children; yes, Father, for such was your gracious will. All things have been handed over to me by my Father, and no one knows the Son except the Father, and no one knows the Father except the Son and anyone to whom the Son chooses to reveal him. Come to me, all who labor and are heavy laden, and I will give you rest. Take my yoke upon you, and learn from me, for I am gentle and lowly in heart, and you will find rest for your souls. (Matthew 11:25-30)

- If the destination of Christlikeness seems too far-fetched, Jesus comes to our rescue. He himself offers to be our guide and instruct us in the kind of life that flows from being with our Creator moment-by-moment.
- We can simultaneously learn from him *and* find rest in him. For example, anyone who has tried to

learn a new language, skill, or life-habit understands the hard work involved. Yet Jesus tells us that when we are hooked-up in right relationship with him we will experience new life and refreshing at the same time. No university in the world can offer that combination.

- Human models of training and leadership depend on intelligence and worldly wisdom for their effectiveness. In this passage the King himself looks heavenward and gives thanks that the kids at the head of the class have no advantage over the rest of the us. In fact, they are in the dark-- God rejoices that human intelligence is inadequate while offering the benefits of relationship to all who will simply come to him. Who wouldn't take a deal like that?

Both these challenges are critical to our personal development as students of Jesus. Our personal spiritual growth depends on coming to terms with these challenges, and the destiny of others depends on our response as well. Plenty of Evangelical churches encourage their people to share the gospel. Few of them call their people to disciple others in the Way. By disconnecting evangelism from discipleship our churches are effectively suggesting to believers that's OK to have spiritual babies and abandon them.

What if our spiritual growth depended upon raising others in the faith? In fact, our spiritual growth depends on that very thing. Any responsible parent can tell you that having children--and raising them--changed their lives for the better. When we look after the development of another person our selfishness dies away. When our concern is for the spiritual success of another we are forced to determine what really works in the Christian life--and what doesn't. Something is missing in us until we make disciples. Something is missing in the world around us when we fail to teach others how to obey everything he commanded us.

### Freely Received, Freely Given

There's only a small difference between the words, "Give what you have," and "Give what you've received," but it's the difference between two kingdoms.

Jesus commissioned his disciples on their very first assignment with these words:

> "As you go, proclaim this message: 'The kingdom of heaven has come near.' Heal the sick, raise the dead, cleanse those who have leprosy, drive out demons. Freely you have received; freely give." Matthew

## 10:7-8

The North American church has been big on the "go, proclaim" part of his instructions: so big, in fact, that in our haste we've sometimes failed to grasp his words, "Freely you have received; freely give." One of the secrets to ministry lies in discovering what you have received before you rush off to give.

These words come from Matthew, chapter 10. It was the first time Jesus sent his disciples out into the field of ministry. Apparently, the Lord considered them prepared--or prepared enough to begin to put their lessons into practice. The disciples had left everything behind to follow Jesus: their businesses as fishermen, their roles as tax collectors, zealots, or whatever had occupied their time before they heard the call, "Come, follow me." The difference between giving what you have and giving what you've received is the difference between the kingdoms of this world and the Kingdom of the age to come. What the disciples received from Jesus was a new way of life. It was the vision of God's Kingdom breaking into the here and now. Let's break it down:

**Give what you have** focuses on our talents, our abilities, and our wealth. The starting point is what we have. We bring not only our resources to the party but also our understanding, methods, and values. One of the telltales of lifeless religion is unhappy people working hard to serve God, bringing the sacrifice of their time, energy and money in a doleful procession. A sign of the Kingdom is people who joyfully share what they've received.

The disciples listened in amazement when Jesus suggested that a rich young ruler should "sell everything you have... then come, follow me." The logic of the world would suggest that a rich man is already poised to serve the King: he need only redirect his wealth toward God, as if God would benefit from deep pockets. In my imagination I see the rich young ruler walking away, shaking his head, thinking, "Jesus missed the boat. I have a lot to offer." Meanwhile Peter speaks up: "we've left everything to follow you." Jesus tells Peter that those who serve him will receive "many times over" what they have given up. I've learned that we not only receive more, but we receive new life: resurrected relationships, resurrected perspective, and resurrected resources.

**Give what you've received** focuses on what God does in us and through us instead of our own abilities. Jesus' instructions to the disciples were simple, and simply impossible: "Heal the sick, raise the dead, cleanse those who have leprosy, drive out demons." Easy, right? In reality,

Jesus gave them a commission that required them to figure out a way to take the Master's presence and power along with them, even when Jesus stayed behind.

A mini-parable: Jesus sent out the twelve to heal the sick, raise the dead, cleanse the lepers, and drive out demons. When they returned the first ten said, "Master, in your name we established hospitals, consoled the grieving, developed a leprosy research institute, and a psychiatric hospital." The other two returned and Jesus asked, "Where are the buildings? How did the fund-raising go?" They answered, "Master, we have none, but we healed the sick, raised the dead, cleansed the lepers, and drove out demons. But we have nothing to show for it."

**What have we received?** Some will dismiss these words as simplistic yearning for signs and wonders, for flash and dazzle. But no: the essence of our calling is to first receive from him--whatever he has to give--and then share his life with others.

Have we ever taken time to sit in silence and reflect on what he has given us? What abilities, insights, anointings or empowerments can we confidently say we have received from Jesus? The passage from Matthew 10 highlights the supernatural, but Jesus has more to give than we imagine. For example, he also said to his friends, "Peace I leave with you;

my peace I give you. I do not give to you as the world gives. Do not let your hearts be troubled and do not be afraid." (John 14:27) Is this a reality for any of us? Then we should share the peace of Jesus with others.

Can you imagine yourself standing next to someone filled with fear, placing your hands upon them, and imparting the peace of Christ? If you've received any measure of peace from him, then it's yours to give. He is the giver of supernatural gifts. He also gives us the fruit of the Spirit: do we have love, joy, peace, patience, kindness, goodness, faithfulness, gentleness and self-control? Then these, too, we should give.

Let's use our imagination one more time: what if each follower of Jesus determined to receive from him each morning, and returned home empty each night. What would the Master say when we returned?

## Making Disciples Makes Me

Christians who readily embrace spiritual formation usually focus on the call to become like Jesus. We embrace the disciplines capable of changing their lives without looking beyond our own welfare in God. But the task of making disciples is central to *our calling* to become like Jesus. We are called to the kind of evangelism that causes us to say, "Be imitators of me, just as I also am of Christ." (1 Corinthians 11:1)

It's not an either/or. It's a both/and. We cannot cloister away from from the world and simply groove on Jesus. Something in us is forever missing if we do not make disciples. Take stock, personally: How would making disciples change *my* walk with God? Following Jesus means discipleship. It's the path to Christlikeness. Part of this path is the change worked in us when we pour our lives into others: we will both will find ourselves changed day-by-day into the image of our common Master.

## CHAPTER THIRTEEN
## SINNERS IN THE HANDS OF WILLY WONKA

Between the efforts of Johnny Depp, Gene Wilder, and Roald Dahl most of us know that five children entered Willy Wonka's chocolate factory one cold British morning and experienced a trial like no other. Before the day's end four of the children were weighed, measured, and found wanting-- their shortcomings revealed to all. The fifth child, Charlie Bucket, was proven kind and virtuous, and received a reward beyond all reason.

The four rejected children were spoiled, each in their own way. They had gone bad the way a peach spoils when left on the kitchen counter too long. In the language of the scripture, these children were sinners.

Wait--did you recoil when you encountered the word sinner? *"Oh no!"* you protest, *"The children had gone bad because their parents had failed them."* Augustus Gloop had been over-fed by a doting mother until he could not control his appetite; Violet Beauregard had been indulged by parents living vicariously through their child; Veruca Salt was a brat because her father had never told her *no;* Mike Teavee was an odious, unruly boy because his parents had surrendered him to the electronic babysitter. No reader (or viewer) could fault Mr. Wonka for separating the children from the factory: he did not give them the chocolate factory because it would have destroyed the children completely and the children would have damaged the factory--along with those who lived and worked there.

These children were, in the very word of Roald Dahl, spoiled. They were not rejected because they broke the house rules, they were sent away because their child-like nature had been corrupted into monstrous distortions of their true potential. Willy Wonka did not follow the children about the factory, rule-book in hand, eager to cite them for any violation. He did not enforce regulations or demand perfection. He simply wanted to give away his creation to those capable of stewarding the factory by the virtue of their heart, a heart in tune with the maker.

The word *spoiled* is useful image for understanding *sin*. The harm of sin is not lawbreaking, but that it mars the image of God in us. Sin spoils us for our true purpose. Sin is not a failure of effort or will, it is a betrayal of our true nature. Sin is bad because it is bad for us, and it makes us bad for those around us. We have, quite literally "gone bad," no longer fit for our highest and best calling. To step into paradise as spoiled brats would ruin us further and perhaps ruin the factory as well.

When we are spoiled (whether by our parents or our own choices) we lose the ability to see God's creation and purpose for what it really is: an invitation to come and live with him forever. We are created to live in harmony with our Maker, but how can we do so if we think him a tyrant, an ogre, or a nit-picking perfectionist? We were created to live in a garden tailored precisely to our needs, but how can we do so if we think our greatest need is to satisfy ourselves at the expense of the garden or our neighbors? He is too good a Father to leave us uncorrected: he wants to make us fit for home again.

When followers of Jesus persist in seeing sin as a violation of the rules they miss the offer of *abundant life*. The Father is not fastidious record-keeper, charting our performance moment by moment. He is, however, a wise caretaker, both of our souls and his world. He longs to free us from sin because it will also release us into a freedom unbefore imagined. He calls us to the perfection of completion that we might drink deeply of the river of life.

James, the brother of Jesus, assures us that "the wisdom that comes from heaven is first of all pure; then peace-loving, considerate, submissive, full of mercy and good fruit, impartial and sincere." (James 3:17) It is the wisdom of obedience: not score-keeping obedience, but obedience that leads to purity and peace.

There is no shortage of golden tickets to admit us to the factory. Our greatest need is to enter unspoiled or renewed, so we can live there forever.

### Dare to Imagine a Life of Harmony:

Some people are realists, others dream. I want to be both kinds of people: first I want to dream, then I want to bring reality to what I've seen. I have a dreambook, more popularly known as the Bible.

Jesus understood the power of imagination and dreams. His teaching invited people to combine *their* thoughts with *his* words and imagine a world born anew. I believe this is how we should listen to the word of God: combine our imagination with his words, producing Biblical dreams of the way things are in heaven and should be on earth:

Consider how the wild flowers grow. They do not

labor or spin. Yet I tell you, not even Solomon in all his splendor was dressed like one of these. If that is how God clothes the grass of the field, which is here today, and tomorrow is thrown into the fire, how much more will he clothe you—you of little faith! And do not set your heart on what you will eat or drink; do not worry about it. For the pagan world runs after all such things, and your Father knows that you need them. But seek his kingdom, and these things will be given to you as well. Do not be afraid, little flock, for your Father has been pleased to give you the kingdom. (Luke 12:27-32)

Can you imagine living a life convinced of the Father's good intentions toward you? How would such a life differ from one in which we worry about our failures or our pressing daily needs? It's like throwing your anchor into the future. With each passing day you are pulled closer to reality, swayed less and less by the currents of this life. But hearing his words requires that we engage our imagination, and see ourselves living such a life right now. It produces hope: Godly hope sprung from a Biblically-informed imagination.

Walter Brueggeman emphasized the idea that our dreams must spring from a source other than our wants and desires. He reminds us we are not free to imagine just anything. We receive the Biblical witness and become invested in the vision. Nor do we do it alone. Brueggeman suggests that the church becomes "a place where people come to receive new materials, or old materials freshly voiced, which will fund, feed, nurture, nourish, legitimate, and authorize a *counterimagination of the world.*"

## Thunderstruck by Power Glory, Goodness, and Promise

Most of us are keenly aware of the qualities we lack as followers of Jesus. We possess the assurance of our weakness instead of the assurance of his faithfulness. The very first believers knew little of such introspection because they directed their gaze toward Jesus. They saw him flash like lightning in the dark sky of human effort. The more clearly they saw him, the more they discovered that his overwhelming love empowered them to become like him.

Here's how Peter explained it:

> "His divine power has given us everything we need for life and godliness through our knowledge of him who called us by his own glory and goodness. Through these he has given us his very great and precious promises, so that through them you may participate in the divine nature and escape the

corruption in the world caused by evil desires. For this very reason, make every effort..." ~ 2 Peter 1:3-5

When I read this passage years ago it flashed like lightning across my heart. I am still thunderstruck by these amazing words. Let's unpack them, phrase by phrase:

"**His divine power...**" As followers of Jesus, our everyday life in Christ is based upon his divine power, not our human strength. Where should we fix our attention--on our lack or on his supply? The life we live reveals the answer of our hearts.

"...**has given us everything we need for life and godliness...**" When was the last time anyone told you that you have everything you need? The beauty of "life and godliness" are within our reach, and has been ever since the resurrection. It's not a "legal fiction," it's a present reality

"...**through our knowledge of him...**" This is a modern road block—our western mindset leads us to believe that the knowledge of him comes through mere study. His first followers knew better: the only true knowledge of him comes as we experience his presence. Apart from his presence we are only spiritual historians.

"... **his own glory and goodness...** " Who talks these days about "glory and goodness?" 21st century Americans have difficulty understanding the glory of God, yet this glory has been streaming live into creation from the very beginning. And his goodness? We walk in that goodness everyday, most of us unaware of this never-ending supply. He is good beyond all measure. Better yet: his glory and goodness are directed toward us!

"**... He has given us very great and precious promises...**" Do we ever reflect upon his promises? Seriously: how many can you name? There are two varieties, those found in the scripture and those he whispers to our hearts. I'm afraid that for most of us his promises are like museum artifacts: beautiful, even curious, but not very useful.

"**... So that through them you may participate in the divine nature...**" Here is where the lightning flash knocked me over. We can participate in God's nature, right here, right now. Who knows the full meaning of this phrase? Not me, but whatever it means, it has to be good!

"**... and escape the corruption in the world caused by evil desires...**" Many believers think the gospel is only about forgiveness, but the good news is even better: corruption is the legacy of a dying world, but we are a new creation.

And still there remains one more. It's not enough to know. We must walk.

**"For this very reason, make every effort..."** Notice that effort comes *after* we encounter his divine power, his glory and goodness, and his precious promises. Too many disciples of Jesus--serious in their commitment to follow him--believe that their effort comes first. Instead, our effort is a response to all he has done: a joyful, grateful, confident recognition of his kindness toward us.

The challenge of this passage continues into verses 5–11, and it is a dangerous challenge at that. The danger of these next verses is that we believe we can accomplish the list apart from his divine power, his glory and goodness, and his precious promises. Only a fool would attempt to fulfill the chain of virtues by human effort alone.

We need the lightning to illuminate the dark landscape of our hearts. We need the thunder to ring in our ears and shake our bones. We need power, glory, goodness, and promise before we take a step. Fortunately, he still thunders forth from heaven.

### Dare to Imagine a Life of Harmony

Like the guy who shows up at a party in 1980's MC Hammer pants, the word, "obedience" is hopelessly out of fashion. The very word *obey* carries with it ridiculous notions of ancient kingdoms, stupid henchmen, or marital imbalance.

*Dis*obedience has always existed, but the idea that our actions should be determined by someone else is passé among North Americans of all kinds: believers and unbelievers alike.

Isaiah dwelt among a "people of unclean lips." We dwell among a people of fierce independence. Our heroes are those who will not bow. I suspect our distrust of obedience flows from our fear of the *other*--the one whom we are to obey. Why should a woman pledge obedience to a husband who is filled with selfishness and pride? Why should a soldier vow obedience to a government pursuing injustice and oppression? Why would anyone put themselves in the hands of another? We are afraid of the other. What agenda does the other person have? To what purpose does someone else demand we do things his way? Following someone else's will exposes us to exploitation and open ourselves to abuse. No one else could possibly have our good as the highest goal. And even if by some crazy chance someone else did have our best interests at heart, how could we be sure they had the wisdom or strength to bring it about?

We refuse to obey because we see the call to obedience as something foreign and alien to our souls. We hear the voice of the Other and put up our defenses because we think something from the outside is trying to invade our lives, our very being. Our life experience has taught us no one could possess the combination of good intentions, perfect wisdom, and effective power to win our trust. We have become convinced we must protect ourselves.

This lies at the heart of our reticence to obey the Heavenly Father. We resist the commands of God because we are not convinced he is good, or his intentions toward us are safe, or he has the wisdom or power to act on our behalf. It is an issue of trust. Church people tell us of his goodness, but our experience and fear tell us otherwise. A drowning man fights against the very lifeguard trying to pull him to shore, but the only answer is submission and harmony with the rescue effort. These are the very things our panic and fear tell us to resist. "Work together with me," says the lifeguard, "and we will get to the shore."

What if the Person who loves us most is also the one capable of showing us how to live? What if the Person who has the wisdom to see life as it really is the very one whispering instructions to our heart? *"This is the way,"* he says, and we feel his breath on our face. *"Walk in it."* What if the one who has infinite power and authority wants to use his strength for our good? Our struggle flows from the fact that the news is too good to believe: the most powerful Being in the universe is also the one who loves us most. We are afraid of power because we have seen its abuse. We distrust good intentions because we are sure no one has the wisdom to navigate the maze of life.

It requires a daring imagination: what if we were created to sing in harmony with the One who writes the perfect song? To resist him would be to resist our own good. To harmonize with him would be to sing the song of life. What if obedience is not the requirement of an alien invasion but an invitation to our highest good? What if a life of submission is actually walking in concert with perfect love? All fear would be gone. Our stumblings would be met with our own desire to get back in step.

There is more good news to believe, even for those of us who call ourselves people of faith. We must dare to believe that the One who loves us most is the truest guide, the surest hand, and fully capable of showing us the way. His way really is the best thing for us. We must see obedience as harmony with the Source of life, not rules and laws and regulations and requirements and chains and bondage. We must discover again that he is the way, the truth, and the life.

### Go Crazy, Order the Happy Meal

Following Jesus sets us up for hard work, right? Study, prayer, meditation, intentional action, and just hunker down to get serious with God. But wait--I thought Jesus said the yoke of discipleship would be easy. What about the light burden? You don't always have to read N.T. Wright. Today, I'm up for a child-like grasp of the scripture. Sometimes simple is better. Consider this famous transformational passage:

> Therefore, I urge you, brothers, in view of God's mercy, to offer your bodies as living sacrifices, holy and pleasing to God--this is your spiritual act of worship. Do not conform any longer to the pattern of this world, but be transformed by the renewing of your mind. Then you will be able to test and approve what God's will is--his good, pleasing and perfect will. (Romans 12:1-2)

Why not enjoy his goodness by taking the easy yoke? Here are four practical suggestions on how to lighten up:

- **Consider his mercies.** What's the use of climbing the mountain if you can't take in the view? After the Apostle Paul has finished all the theological heavy-lifting of the first eleven chapters of Romans, he urges us to take a look at the mercies of God. Why not ask God to open your eyes to his mercies? They're new every morning.

- **Offer your body.** He made our hands and called them good. They are holy when we set them aside for him. Sometimes it's a good idea to simply hold our hands in front of the Almighty and say, "Here, use mine."

- **Become a non-conformist.** Declare your independence from everyday patterns and change things up. Go crazy: order the Happy Meal. I know it's trite, and clearly Paul's point is much larger, but sometimes the simple act of breaking the patterns in our everyday lives can open us up to a new, Spirit-inspired perspective.

- **Trade in your brain.** The "renewing of your mind" doesn't always have to come from deep study. Sometimes it can come from deep breathing. Make room for the Spirit: give your thoughts a rest. Have you ever noticed the phrase *"be transformed"* is passive?

This passage has launched untold hard-working disciples--and seen eager disciples fall short of their best intentions. No less an authority than Dallas Willard commented, "The idea 'no pain, no gain,' well... that's just something a football coach thought up."

You can sweat it out tomorrow. Today? Let the wind of the Spirit mess up your hair.

# CHAPTER FOURTEEN
## THE CHURCH: HIGH EXPECTATIONS, NO ILLUSIONS

Once, somewhere in the Northern Highlands, among the hills of rock, two masons set out to build their homes. In the thin light of a new Spring morning, they each gathered stones together for their task.

The first mason selected stones suited for the work. He carted them to his site and quickly joined them together into a house both sturdy and safe. Because he finished his work quickly he built another house. And another. And still another until the landscape was filled with houses of stone, all sturdy and safe, but each one cold and empty.

The second mason made a curious choice of building materials, for among the Highlands was a quivering mountain of *living stones*. These stones were no bigger than those used by the first mason. They were no stronger or better shaped, nor any more lovely than the others. But they were *alive*: they spoke, they sang, they even argued, and somehow they could move of their own accord, even after being selected by the second mason. As the mason piled the living stones into his wagon they asked where he was taking them. When they saw the plans for his house some cheered and sang while others complained and wandered away. They wanted no part of his house. Still the mason joined the stones together, building the walls and arches and hearth of a home fit for his purpose.

But because he had chosen living stones, the house was never completed. Some stones jumped from the cart before they arrived at the building. The work was forever unfinished as the mason returned to the mountain quarry again and again for more supply. Other stones allowed the mason to place them in the wall but failed to connect with the wall-mates on their left and right: they argued, they cried, and when they had could stand it no more, they left.

Still he continued to build. Always the house was incomplete. Some mornings the Mason would return to work only to discover that the stones had re-arranged themselves in the night. The Mason made curious choice to leave holes in the walls where the stones had fled, because (he said) "I selected that stone and crafted a place for it alone. Another cannot take it's place."

From time to time a missing stone would wander back to the house and the Mason lovingly fitted it back in the wall again. Some stones stayed in place forevermore, but some left (and returned) time and again. Still he continued to build. Room upon room he added, not one of them finished until there grew an unwieldy mansion both large and incomplete. In this mansion he chose to live, year after year in fellowship with the living stones that breathed in every wall.

Passers-by would stop and stare in amazement. Many laughed at the sprawling mess of a mansion that had grown on the landscape. It seemed without design and devoid of all reason.

"Why don't you use the stones all the other masons use?" they laughed. "You could finish your house in days and be done with the work."

"This building *is* my work," replied the Second Mason. "And as for the living stones it is true--they are a bother: but I could never build with dead ones, for this is my home, and I've come that they might have life."

## There Is More

My Dad used to believe some crazy things about me. Every so often he would tell me I could do anything. He said I was smart and funny. He thought I could beat up any kid in my class. It was comical because I was the pee-wee of the school who ran his mouth way too much and then hid behind the teacher's skirt. Clearly, my father didn't live in the same world as I did.

I was convinced my father had no clue about my life, so I ignored his advice. Years later, when I came to the pages of the New Testament I began to hear the same voice urging me to lift my vision. Over the years I've heard that voice at least four times. It's talking to all of us, not just me.

**"God had planned something better for us so that only together with us would they be made perfect."** (Hebrews 11:40) After describing incredible heroes of faith, the writer of Hebrews turns his attention to us. Compared to all those other guys in the Bible, God has planned something better for us. There's more. And it's better. And it's for us. wilder still: the stuff God has planned for us completes the faith of those from ages past. Are you kidding me? Something is lacking in the experiences of Abraham, Isaac, Jacob, Joseph, and well, the whole list—and they are looking to us for the fulfillment of their experiences? No wonder there is a great cloud of witnesses looking on.

**"His intent was that now, through the church, the manifold wisdom of God should be made known to the rulers and authorities in the heavenly realms."** (Ephesians 3:10) To begin with, I have no clear idea who the "rulers and authorities in the heavenly realms" are, but when God wants to put his wisdom on display, he points at the church. Are you kidding me? I love my local church, but it hardly reaches the level of manifesting all of God's wisdom. God points at us, and we turn around as if he's pointing at someone behind us.

**"I tell you the truth, anyone who has faith in me will do what I have been doing. He will do even greater things than these, because I am going to the Father."** (John 14:12) Are you kidding me? Is he really talking about us? When Jesus opens up with "I tell you the truth" it means, "read my lips, this is serious." Still stranger--his words are in the singular: "anyone" and "he." My favorite rationalization about this verse used to be that Jesus was talking about the aggregate works of all believers in all times: but there's no way you can read it like that. He means me, and then he means you. This is the sort of verse that causes me to raise my eyes toward Heaven and say, "Surely, you're joking." Jesus predicted a church filled with individuals, each one capable of doing the works he did.

**"His divine power has given us everything we need for life and godliness through our knowledge of him who called us by his own glory and goodness."** (2 Peter 1:3) The reason I have so much trouble with this verse is that it lays so much responsibility at my feet. Everything for life and godliness? Are you kidding me? He's given us everything we need? Well then, go get 'em. This is a challenge personally, but an even bigger challenge together. We *have* all we need, but apparently we all have the supply as well, so what's stopping us?

My Dad may not have been a part of my childhood world, but my God knows this world better than I do. My natural father spoke to me out of parental hope and pride. Our Heavenly Father speaks to us out of transcendent truth. Why don't we listen more often?

### Forget it, I'm going to the Pub

It's difficult to be in favor of the church when the church has let so many people down. The trail of disappointment leads right to our door, because each of us has experienced the failings of the church. Nearly everyone has stories of small-minded, mean-spirited people who use the church as an opportunity to act as if they are God's gift to Christendom. So forget it. I give up. Jesus and I can hang out together at my house. I can meet him at Starbucks. Or the pub.

And yet…

Jesus looked into the centuries and saw a bride. The inspired scripture makes outrageous statements about the church, outrageous enough to bring me to the edge of unbelief. Like parenting, I marvel that Jesus would leave something so important in the hands of people so messed up. It's a heckuva way to run a railroad, but it's his operation, not mine. This is the chapter when some will jump off the train, because it's about the importance of the church for every student of Jesus. But wait--it gets worse, because the text on my mind is one that's been used to beat people over the head regarding church attendance:

Let us not give up meeting together, as some are in the habit of doing, but let us encourage one another—and all the more as you see the Day approaching. (Hebrews 10:25)

Can this blunt instrument of condemnation be redeemed? Is there more to this passage than a club for the small-minded to thump the rest of us? I believe so, because verse 25 does not stand alone, it lives among a string of *"Let Us"* statements reaching back to Hebrews 10:22:

> Let us draw near to God with a sincere heart in full assurance of faith, having our hearts sprinkled to cleanse us from a guilty conscience and having our bodies washed with pure water. Let us hold unswervingly to the hope we profess, for he who promised is faithful. And let us consider how we may spur one another on toward love and good deeds. Let us not give up meeting together, as some are in the habit of doing, but let us encourage one another—and all the more as you see the Day approaching. (Hebrews 10:22-25, there: that's better!)

I invite you to consider the larger message of Hebrews 10 with these five observations:

- **Let us draw near to God (v 22):** Jesus has done his part. Now it's up to us to respond. "Draw near" is the first of the "let us" statements, and "meeting together" comes second to last. Do we see the connection? One sure way to draw near to God is to come together with his family. But a word of caution: we should draw near with with a clean heart and a free conscience. We are commanded to draw near; we are not commanded to surrender to guilt, manipulation or hype of the those who would use church life for their own purposes.

- **Let us hold unswervingly to hope (v 23):** Students of Jesus carry hope. We are called to speak words of hope. Imagine coming together with others filled with hope, each on eager to "profess" their hopes out loud. The world knows the difference between hope and hype: one attracts, the other repels.

- **Let us consider how we may spur one another on towards love and good deeds (v 24):** What a crazy image comes with the word, "spur." Imagine a horseback rider giving her heels to the horse. Another translation suggests "provoke one another." Here's a crazy-evil Christian meditation: before I head for church I should ask, "have I plotted some way to provoke others to love and good deeds?" Conversely, who will be there to spur me on toward my calling to represent the grace of God? Remember, though-- I've got a clean conscience and I'm not buying guilt, so the only way to provoke me is to demonstrate the real thing.

- **Let us not give up meeting together (v25):**
Apparently there were reasons way back then to
give up on the church, which means that in our
day we haven't stumbled into some new
revelation about jumping off the train. The
additional challenge is the word, "meeting."
Church meetings back then may not resemble the
form we have, but whatever it looked like it was
regular and organized. When people say, "I don't
like organized religion," what's the alternative,
disorganized religion? Do we think the Holy
Spirit is incapable of organizing more than two
or three people?

- **Let us encourage one another (25):** This final
suggestion cuts to the heart of the matter--is your
church a place of encouragement, or guilt? Does
your church move in the vision of God's
awesome future or do they trade in hype that
can't last until Thursday? And of course, there's
the little matter of the word, "us." Who carries
the encouragement? Who has the vision? Do we
go to church like we go to WalMart--to pick up
inexpensive cheer--or do we go to church as

vessels of hope and encouragement, ready to spill ourselves all over the place?

These five points are a call for us to move beyond obedience to vision, to move beyond following the rules of the Bible to capturing the heart of Jesus. He sees something in the church we do not. Which one of us needs the eye exam?

### Beyond Mere Community:

Many will object. We all have tales of hypocrites, self-righteous blowhards, and sexual predators. I get it. The North American church is desperately sick, and in many cases the church hinders the spiritual growth of believers. But before we all decide have coffee and croissants down the street with the cool kids and call it church, we'd better think clearly about what makes a "church." I'd like to suggest that God has given us a few clues about what He thinks makes up a church. The bottom line is: church is God's idea, complete with certain criteria as to what makes us a church. We ignore them at our peril.

It's a book-length discussion--a life-length discussion, actually--but here is one man's list of at least six vital parts of a real church:

- **The church meets together regularly**: Sunday morning isn't the only possibility. In fact, Acts 2:42-47 suggests they met together far *more* than North Americans might find comfortable. In a variety of settings, for a multitude of reasons, followers of Jesus meet together regularly and share their lives together. The regular, habitual gathering is a mark of the church.

- **The church has a defined structure:** Structure is built into God's order of creation. Single-celled organisms reveal astonishing complexity of function; in the human body there is individualized function. Without the structure of a skeleton, the body cannot stand. These physical realities point toward spiritual truth. Amazingly, the scripture seems to endorse a *variety* of church structures, but every New Testament church had a recognizable structure. We can disagree on what that structure may look like, but it's not possible to read Acts or the Epistles without recognizing it's importance.

- **The church provides authority:** Authority! Just mention the word and people tense up. Abuses abound, guilt is common currency, and the church in North America differs little from any business down the street. Yet we all must personally come to terms with passages like, "Obey your leaders and submit to their authority." (Hebrews 13:17) Paul's letters to Timothy and Titus could be considered all about authority! Nearly everyone has a horror-story about abuse of authority in the church. Here's my take: authority without compassion and relationship makes a sham of God's Kingdom, but compassion and relationship without authority miss God's Kingdom entirely.

- **The church is a proving ground for love and forgiveness.** "Therefore, as God's chosen people, holy and dearly loved, clothe yourselves with compassion, kindness, humility, gentleness and patience. Bear with each other and forgive whatever grievances you may have against one another. Forgive as the Lord forgave you. And over all these virtues put on love, which binds them all together in perfect unity." (Colossians 3:12-14) These words are *impossible* to live out in isolation. I believe the Father designed families and churches as the venues for love and forgiveness. How can we live out these words apart from our families, or the church--which is the family of God?

- **The church equips God's people.** Christian maturity requires a nurturing family atmosphere. Gifts of the Holy Spirit and the development of Christian character thrive in a healthy community. Entertainment apart from equipping is antithetical to God's plan for the church--there are plenty of churches that amount to nothing more than TV shows. But fellowship and community without equipping also falls short of the mark. If there's no equipping going on, it's not fully the church. Jesus is into lab, not lecture. And it's not recess, either.

- **The church provides a unique corporate witness:** There have been exceptional individuals throughout history. Saints and geniuses appear larger than life, and because they are are so exceptional they are easily dismissed as individuals, even freaks. But who could dismiss an entire community of faith? "A new command I give you: Love one another. As I have loved you, so you must love one another," said Jesus in

John 13:34 "By this all men will know that you are my disciples, if you love one another." The early church would either get you healed or care for you until you died. Widows, orphans and outcasts of the first century knew there was a refuge called "the church."

Object if you will: it's easy to do. The church has failed in every area. This list is not meant as a defense of the way things are. Jesus has a vision for his gathered people. Perhaps this list is a start.

Some things should change--and I believe the change begins with us as individuals. If you must leave your current church, then go. But where? If you can find a group of believers attempting to fulfill these six ideals you will land in a safe place. Leaving a sick church may be the best decision. Ignoring God's plan for your personal growth as a disciple never is.

### What I Saw at Church

Yesterday at church I saw heaven breaking into earth here and now.

I saw signs and wonders: children in sparkling tennis shoes that flashed multicolored lights as they danced in worship. I saw a four year-old offensive lineman soaking in the Spirit of Christ, unaware of how strong his body will grow or how he will use it to glorify God. I saw the Woodstock generation worshipping next to generations unborn. I saw the unlovely, enraptured by the bridegroom and made beautiful by the sight of of him. They became beautiful in my sight as well. I saw a rage-o-holic find peace as he stood in the back of the room. He drank it in--the only peace he knows each week--in the Father's presence.

I heard voices normally used in the everyday business of life blended together in the unison of praise. Voices which sang without words, making new paths of melody, expressing what their hearts knew but their minds did not. I heard songs so new that no one had ever heard them but the singer herself, followed by the songs of saints dead a hundred years or more. I heard the sound of heaven surge through tongues, lungs, and throats of flesh and blood, like fountains made pure by the very water they released.

I tasted bad coffee. It was somehow made better because it was shared in common. I savored the sacred elements of donuts and fruit, muffins and juice, sanctified by people receiving the sacrament of family. I tasted and saw that the Lord is good. I caught the fragrance of the unwashed who had been embraced by the Rose of Sharon. I discovered that his aroma overpowers theirs: the aroma of life to those who are being saved, and the stench of death nowhere in the place.

I heard the Holy Spirit whisper secrets to the pastor, who announced them to the church. I watched as the people miraculously flashed the inspired words around the world even before the sermon had ended. I saw sojourners who had no home find a place to call home, if only for an hour.

I saw in the church the fullness of him who fills every thing in every way. I discovered the pillar and support of the truth as they put the wisdom of God on display--not for themselves, but for the powers and principalities in heavenly places--unaware they were being watched.

Yesterday at church I touched all these things and more. What did you see?

Made in the USA
San Bernardino, CA
21 January 2016